Pemaquid Papers.

PAPERS
Relating to
PEMAQUID
and parts adjacent in the preſent ſtate of Maine, known as

CORNWALL COUNTY,
WHEN UNDER THE

COLONY OF NEW-YORK,

Compiled from Official Records in the office of the Secretary of State at Albany, N. Y.

BY

FRANKLIN B. HOUGH.

ALBANY,
Weed, Parſons & Companie.

MDCCCLVI.

INDEX.

INTRODUCTION.

THE obſcurity which has involved the hiſtory of that portion of Maine included within the patent of the Duke of York, while under the ducal government, has long been felt and acknowledged,[1] and hiſtorians in their accounts of this period, have been obliged in the abſence of authentic documents, to rely upon ſlight and imperfect data. The following papers now for the firſt time printed, it is believed, will add much to our acquaintance with the annals of the ſection known as "*Pemaquid and its dependencies*," in the early records of New-York.

The dependance of a part of Maine upon the government of New-York, originated as follows: William Alexander, Earl of Sterling, Secretary of the kingdom of Scotland, having been previouſly concerned in extenſive grants in Nova Scotia[2]

[1] Vide, Williamſon's Hiſt. of Maine, i, 228 et ſeq.—Coll. of Maine Hiſt. Soc., ii, 229–237:—ib. iv, 209, &c.

[2] The Nova Scotia Charter was granted March 9, 1621, confirmed and enlarged by a second patent, Sept. 10, of the ſame year. Williamſon's Hiſt. of Maine, i, 223—Sullivan's Hiſt. of Maine, 124—Coll. of Maine Hiſt. Soc., i, 11.

and in the operations of the Plymouth Company, received by lot, in 1635,[1] one of the three divisions into which the territory of Maine was divided upon the dissolution of that Company. The share thus received, extended from the Kennebeck to the St. Croix rivers, and embraced several grants previously made, upon which settlements had been commenced.

In 1663, the Earl of Clarendon, on behalf of the Duke of York, purchased of Henry, then Earl of Sterling, his interest in American grants,[2] including, besides that of Maine, the title of Long Island, Nantucket, Martha's Vineyard,[3] and other islands adjacent, and in 1664,[4] the Duke of York received from his Royal brother a Charter for these territories and

[1] These lots were drawn Feb. 3, the grants executed April 22, and the charter of the company surrendered June 7, of that year. Coll. of Maine Hist. Soc., i, 42–44—Coll. of New Jersey Hist. Soc., ii, 38.

[2] The consideration of this purchase was £3,500, but upon failure of payment, a life annuity of £300 was, in 1674, agreed upon, payable out of the net profits of revenue arising from the colony, which proving insufficient, an order was issued in 1689 for the arrears to be paid out of the funds of the Colony. New-York Coll. Hist., iii, 606.

[3] A small edition of a volume embracing the New-York official records concerning Nantucket and adjacent islands, prepared by the editor of this volume, has been printed under the patronage of the Hon. John V. L. Pruyn, of Albany, for distribution among public libraries.

[4] March 12, Vide Patents, i, 109, Secretary's Office, Albany.

others, then held by the Dutch, ſince known as New-York, New Jerſey and Delaware.

The New-York records do not ſhow what juriſdiction was aſſerted over the eaſtern portion of the Duke's territories prior to the reduction of New-York by the Dutch in 1673. Upon that occaſion the General Court of Maſſachusetts, under pretext of a ſurvey that included the territory, took poſſeſſion of the Pemaquid ſettlements, organized a local government,[1] and in July, 1674, a court was held under this authority within the Duke's territories. Upon the reſtoration of New-York to the Engliſh, by the peace of Weſtminſter,[2] a new patent, embracing the ſame territory, was taken out by the Duke of York,[3] and upon the arrival of governor Androſs, meaſures were taken to re-eſtabliſh this authority throughout the government. Civil and military commiſſions were iſſued, and upon the organization of a General Aſſembly in New-York in 1683, and

[1] Williamſon's Hiſt. of Maine, i, 443—Coll. of Maine Hiſt. Soc., i, 131.

[2] Feb. 9, 1674, Art. 6.

[3] June 29, 1674, Vide Smith's Hiſt. of New-York, (1814) 61—Dunlap's Hiſt. of New-York, i, 129.

the divifion of the colony into counties, "Pemy-Quid, and all the Territories in thofe Parts, with the Iflands adjacent," were erected into the county of *Cornwall*, and entitled to fend one member to the General Affembly.[1] This connection continued until the fucceffion of the Duke of York to the throne, when by a royal order[2] thefe territories were annexed to the New England government.

The following papers are arranged chronologically, with references to the originals in the New-York Secretary's office. The occurrence of a line of afterifks, denotes an omiffion of matter relating to other fubjects, and a row of periods, indicates a lofs of part of the record. The original orthography has been followed, except in the ufe of capital initials in names of perfons, where fmall letters had been employed.

[1] Nov. 1, 1683. Orig. Laws, MSS. ii.—Livingfton & Smith's, &c., Ed. Laws, i, 6.—The act organizing counties was re-enacted Oct. 1, 1691. It will be feen that Gyles Goddard actually reprefented Cornwall county during one feffion.

[2] This order was dated Sept. 19, 1686, Deeds viii, 75, Secretary's office, Albany.

PAPERS RELATING TO
PEMAQUID
AND ITS DEPENDENCIES.

EXTRACT from the Grant to the Duke of York, Dated 12*th March Ao* 16. *Car.* 2.*d* 1664.

[Patents i. 109.]

CHARLES the Second by the Grace of God King of England Scotland ffrance & Ireland Defender of the ffaith &c To all to whom theſe p'nts ſhall come Greeting: Know yee that wee for diverſe good Cauſes and Conſideracõns us thereunto moving Have of our eſpeciall Grace Certaine knowledge and meere motion Given and Granted And by theſe preſents for us our heires and ſucceſſo^{rs} Do Give and Grant unto our Deareſt Brother James Duke of Yorke his heires and Aſſignes All that part of the Maine Land of New England begining at a Certaine place called or knowne by the name of St Croix, next adjoyning to New Scotland in America and from thence extending along the ſea coaſt unto a certaine place called Petuaquine or Pemaquid and ſo up the River thereof to the furtheſt head of y^e^ ſame as it tendeth northwards and extending from thence to the River Kinebequi, and ſo upwards by the ſhorteſt courſe to the River Canada northwards: And alſo * * * *

[Here follows a grant for the province of New-York and parts of Maſſachuſetts and Connecticut, New Jersey, Delaware, &c.]

Lre to ye Inhabitants of Pemaquid.

[General Entries iv. 258.]

GENTS. It might ſeem ſtrange to you that in ſoe long diſtance of time thoſe parts under his Royall Highness Patronage and Protection, of which you are Membrs & Inhabitants have not been aſſumed in any particular care & Governmt. as Subſtitute to his Royall Highness, by whoſe Grace and Indulgence I am (under him) appointed Governo[r]. of all his Territoryes in America; And truly I might juſtly have fallen under yor Cenſure of Remiſſ-ness, were I not allwayes in Expectacõn that Affayres would have been perfected by my worthy Predeceſſo[r] Coll: Nicolls, to whom the ſole managery of that Busy-ness was committed; neither could I ever doubt of the perfecting of it, had it not been interrupted by an Active & furious warr, in wch Expedition hee moſt ſadly, (yet as bravely) laid down his Life at his Masters ffeet;[1] All expectations from him being now wholly extinct, It is a Duty incumbent on mee to erect a ſuperſtructure on that ffoundation, which hee in his Lifetime worthily aimed at; To which end I ſhall deſire you, ffirſt to give mee a true ſtate of yo[r] Affayres, as they now ſtand; next That you would tranſmitt to mee a modell of ſuch a Governm[t]. as ſhall bee moſt conducing to the Happyness of that Colony, both to its ſafety Traffick, & Increaſe of Inhabitants, promiſing upon the reception of that Scheme, not only

[1] Coll. Richard Nicolls was ſlain in a naval engagement with the Dutch, in the ſervice of the Duke of York, in 1672. A monument is erected to his memory in Amphil Church, Bedfordſhire, England.

to Inveſt you wth ample power to Exerciſe yor Authority both to Eccleſiaſtick as Civill Affayres, but will bee ready on all Occaſions to bee aſſiſting to you in the Preſervation of all yor Rights and Intereſt againſt any ſiniſter Obſtructions; Thus deſiring to heare from you by the firſt Opportunity, I heartily recommend you to the Allmighty's Protection, & remaine

Yo^{r} Very Affectionate ffriend,

FRAN: LOVELACE.

Fort James on ye Iſland Manhatans
in N: Yorke, ffeb: 16th 167$\frac{2}{3}$.

Council Minutes.

[Council Minutes vol iii. Part II. Page 117.]

At a Councell Sept 8th 1676.

Preſent The Governo^{r}
Capt Brockhols The Secretary
Capt Dyre.

* * * *

A Letter coming from Boſton to the Governor from Mr Abr Corbetts who lives to the Eaſtward, in the Dukes Patent, relateing the deſtruction of the Eaſtern parts near Pemaquid &c by ye Indians, in the month of Aug^ſt^ laſt, about the 20th day of the month, The ſame being read and conſidered of,

Reſolved, to ſend a ſloope to Piſcataway Salem and Boſton, to invite and bring as many of the Inhabitants particularly ffiſhermen as will come driven from the Dukes Territoryes, and parts Eaſtward, and to ſupply them with Land in any part of the Government they ſhall chuſe.

* * * *

[New-York Colonial MSS. xxvii.]

At a Councell held in N. Y. the 5th day of Jan 1677.

Vpon a L^re^ from the Go: of Boſton dated No: 13th brought hither by Mr Wm Bowdiſh the 2^d^ inſt. deſiring and order for the delivery of the Ketches at Pemaquid, to their own^rs^, of which ſaid Mr Bowditch with Mr Wm Duvall is ſaid to be oner, And the ſaid Mr Bowditch on y^e^

behalfe of himſelfe & Mr Duvall offering ſecurity to pay ſalvage or what other Charges their Ketch ſhall be adjudged unto by the Go: alleadging alſo that the ſd Ketch lyeing at ſhee doth will bee quite spoyled, & alſo will looſe the fiſhing ſeaſon this ſpring for which they make ready in ffebr, & is comonly eſteemed to bee worth double yt it is the reſt of the yeare.

The ſame being particularly taken into conſideracõn

Reſolved That an order be given to ye ſd Mr Bowditch on behalfe of himſelfe & Mr Duvall for the delivery of the ſd Ketch unto him or whom hee ſhall appoint, hee giving ſecurity to the value of the Ketch here to pay ſalvage, or ſuch other charges as ſhee ſhall bee adjudged unto, at the returne of the Governor

An order hereupon for the delivery

A bond of 400lb for paymt of 200

Tho Del: & Wm Bowditch of Salem.

Wm Bowditch of Salem in N: Engl Merch & Tho Delavall of New-Yorke Merch a blank ſum bound to Edm Andros Eſq Go. in this his R H. Territoyes in America his Succeſſor & Aſſignes.

(The foregoing paper was endorſed as follows:)

To Capt Caeſar Knapton, Comand[r]

You are hereby deſired to cauſe the Ketch . . . . . of . . . . to bee deliuered unto M[r] W[m] Bowditch or his order, according to the order of Council hereunto annexed hee having given in ſufficient ſecurity for the doing whereof this ſhall bee yo[r] diſcharge

Given under my hand the 7th day of January 1677

Copie of a Letter to the Go: of Boſton.

N. Y. Jan 7. 1677.

[New-York Colonial MSS. xxvii.]

Ho[BLE] S[R].

Yo.[rs] of No:[r] 13.th by M.[r] Bowditch, directed to our Go: or in his abſence to his dep: arrived not here till the 2[d] inst, which was almoſt 6. weekes after his departure, The contents whereof relate to the delivery of the Ketches at Pemaquid to the Owners, Its ſuppoſed you meane the former owners, Otherwiſe ye fortune of the warre had apparently made them change Maſt.^{rs} It could have beene right, thoſe perſons had made their claymes or applicacõn for them ſoon^{r}, probably ere this they had from Comãnder Knapton, but ſeverall Reports comĩng that ſome of thoſe own^{rs} have ſ^{d} they had rather the Indyans had kept their Ketches, then that they ſhould come into the hands of New-Yorke Governm^{t} might in part bee the occaſion why no other order was ſent thither, then for their apprizem^{t}, and not broſt here the rugged winter ſeaſon ſetting in ſeeming to forbid their removall till spring,

Your opinion about the delivery of the veſſels as well as captives, which you underſtand by the Go:^{r} Letter, to bee mentioned in the peace, ſeemes to bee followed with ſome paſſion in the following clauſe, that if they were not delivered for the benefitt of the right Own^{rs} that loſt them, you ſhould not know to underſtand his mocõns, for I ſuppoſe they will appeare to have tended to ye Gen.^{all} good of his

Maties ſubjects in thoſe parts as well as the intereſts of the Governm[t], & will always bee our aime to act with charity and juſtice towards o[r] neighbo[rs]. as well as others, & which we could have the like retaliation from them, then ſhould wee not bee ſo often Cenſured & Condemned:

It cannot but bee admited that you ſo often repeate the overtures of peace betweene us & y[e] Indyans wrote to you of from Pemaquid, as you ſay & that unleſſe the veſſels were d[d]. as well as captives you ſhould not comply on any other termes, ſince if you will againe peruſe o[r] Letters you will find that the concluſion wee had made was a poſitive peace beyond any overtures or ceſſacõn of Armes, & our ſending to you, was onely to acquaint you, that we had as neighbo[rs]: & ſubjects to one Pr. encluded you if you pleaſed, and if you had refuſed it, upon any nice termes not comprehended in the Agreem[t]. wee had made, the prejudice would have redounded to your ſelves, & allthough afterwards by a collaterall Agreem[t]. wee got the Ketches to bee encluded, it was not becauſe you mentioned you otherwiſe ſhould not comply &c., but out of a deſire to the publick Good of his Ma[ties] ſubjects, without any private aymes or pretence of particular advantage otherwiſe:

The which that you may find will bee made Good by deeds as well as words, I have with the advice of the Councell upon the application from M[r] Bowditch given order for the delivery of the Ketch wherein hee is conſerned hee giving ſecurity to anſwer what ſalvage or other charges there may be adjudged unto at the Go: returne, which you may bee confid.[t] will not bee unreaſonable. And in any . . . . elſe ſhall not bee wanting to continue fr . . . correſpondence with o[r] neighbo[rs] being

Ho:[ble] S.[r]

Yo.[r] moſt humble Serv.[t]

N. Y. Jan. 7. 1677. A. B.[1]

[Council Minutes vol iii. Part II. Page 153.]

At a Councell June 9, 1677.

A propoſall being made by the Governor whether it would bee adviſable to

[1] Anthony Brockholls.

ſend to take Poſſeſſion and aſſert the Dukes Intereſt at Pemaquid, & parts adjacent Eaſtward, according to his Roy[ll] H[s] Pattent or nott,

Upon conſideracõn had thereupon, It was thought adviſeable ſo to do, And that if we make Peace with the Indyans there the Maſſachuſetts to bee comprized if they Pleaſe.

All the ffiſhermen & old inhabitants to be reſtored and Protected.

* * * *

[New-York Colonial MSS. xxvii.]

To Cap[t] Anthony Brockholes & the Reſt of y[e] Councell of y[e] Government of New-Yorke.

The Humble Peticõn of William Bowditch of Salem in New Engl[d] Merch[t]

Sheweth.

That yo[r] Pet[r] being bound for Pemaquid in the month of March paſt, to receive his Ketch, brought there by the

Indyans, for ye which he had an Order of Councell, he made purchaſe from the Owners of two other Ketches lying there, that had likewiſe been brought in by the ſaid Indyans, which ſaid Ketches, if ſome ſpeedy care bee not taken about them will be altogether ſpoyled & uſeleſſe, haveing layd hall'd up in a Creeke all this winter, where they are alſo subject to the Hazard of being fired, by ſome malicious Indyan of whome there is too much ſuſpicõn.

You^r Pet^r doth therefore moſt humbly prai, that hee may have an Order to be poſſeſſt of the ſ^d two Ketches, in like manner as hee had for the former, & hee ſhall give ſecurity to pay all ſuch ſalvage and charges as they ſhall be adjudged to pay, at the returne of the Governo.^r

And yor pet^n will ever pay &c.

[Council Minutes iii. Part II. 163.]

At a Councell 2^d Augs^t 1677

Capt Brockholes &c Lett^rs from Pemaquid of 12th & 13th of July read.

Ordered ſending to or ſeeking the Indyans not allowable, but if they apply &

ſubmitt according to the Inſtruccõns to bee received, for any Particulars, may apply to the Governo^{r} at New Yorke, for wch on their Deſire to finde them paſſage in ſome of our ſloops going & returning.

Orders, and Inſtructions to bee very punctually and ſtrictly Obſerved particularly that none on any Pretence whatever, doe range or goe into the woods or creeks, but to uſe all endeavours to ſecure the Open Sea Coaſts and Iſlands as well as defend the ffortt.

To admitt or treat with no p^{r}ſons whatever but upon all Occaſions or applicacõns to refferr to the Governo at New Yorke.

Another Sloope to bee forthwth ſent with ye above Orders and a further Supply of Stores for the Garriſon.

The Garriſon being ſettled that Capt Brockholes or Enſigne Knapton bee left with fiffty ſoldiers and the Sloopes Company the other Offic^{rs} to Come home as p^{r} former Intimacõn in the Governo^{rs} Lett^{r} the 26th paſt.

Any difference betweene Inhabitants and ffiſhermen to bee determined by M^{r}

Joſeline, or other Juſtice of the Peace but in extraordinary Caſes of great Import or value ye commander to be p^r^ſent, and appeale allowed to the Governo^r^ and Councell at Yorke if deſired according to Law.

[Councell Minutes iii. Part II. 169.]

At a Councell Sep^t^ 11th 1677.

Reſolved that no Inhabitants bee admitted to dwell in his R^ll^ H^s^ Territories at Pemaquid and parts adjacent.

The Indyans there upon their ſubmiſſion admitted and Confirmed to live as other Indyans of the Goverm^t^, they comporting themſelves, and living as they ought.

The trading place to be at Pemaquid & no where elſe.

All Entryes to bee made att New Yorke and no Coaſters or Interlopers allow'd but if any found to be made prize.

All Engliſh ffiſhers to have free liberty of ffiſhing, they conforming themſelves to ſuch orders & rules as ſhall be given for the benefitt of ſaid ffiſhery.

Liberty of Stages upon the ffiſhing Iſlands but not upon the Maine except at Pemaquid neare the ffortt.

The Indyans not to goe to y^e ffiſhing Iſlands.

No rum to bee dranke on that ſide the ffort ſtands.

No man to truſt any Indyans.

* * * * *

At a Councell Sept 27. 1677

* * * * *

$Lett^{rs}$ from Pemaquid from Mr Caeſar Knapton Commander at Pemaquid, & the ffrench att St Johns, & Penobſcott read.

Orders and Directions for the Commander att Pemaquid.

[Warrants Orders Paſſes &c iii. 268.]

The Indyans late ſubmiſſion and peace with them admitted and allow'd and comporting themſelves as they ought, to have all Juſtice, and freedome of living neare, converſe and commerſe with us, as all other Indyans of the Government have and do enjoy.

Butt to prevent all Inconveniency's or occasions of difference, no Indyans to goe to the fishing Islands, nor Christians admitted or suffer'd to inhabit or converse on the Maine, except att Pemaquid under protection of the Fort, this winter, or till further Order, to which place supplys are and shall be sent for all partys.

Traders from Yorke and that bring sufficient clearings from the Custome house according to act of Parliament, to be admitted to sett up for the present trading houses, under command, butt att convenient distance from the Fort, to the Landward, so as a street be left of good breadth, directly from the Fort to the narrowest part of the neck or point of land the Fort stands upon, going to the great neck towards New Harbour; and if endwise should any wayes blind, or hinder the fort of the sight or command of the water, then said houses to be sett broadways to the said designed street, to which all Doores to open, and not suffer'd on any other side or End.

All trade to be in the said Street, in or afore the houses, between sun and sun, for which the drum to beate, or bell ring every morning & evening, and neither Indyan nor Chriſtian ſuffer'd to drinke any ſtrong drinke, nor lye aſhore in the night, upon the neck or Point of land the Fort ſtands upon, & any preſuming to the contrary or coming there drunk to bee apprehended and puniſhed according to his deſert, and allſo all Traders not giving over, and immediately ſhutting their doors att ſaid time and warning.

No Indyans nor Chriſtians to be Admitted att any time within the Fort except ſome few upon occaſion of buſineſſe below, but none to goe up into the Redout, nor no manner of trade whattever, upon any accompt or pretence whattsoever att no time in or neare the Fort, butt in the above ſtreet, upon penalty of forſeiture of all such traders Goods and priviledge and Corporall puniſhment as the caſe may deſerve.

Fiſhermen giving notice to the Fort, to have all Liberty of making their fiſh on the fiſhing Iſlands, or neare and under the protection of the Fort.

If Occaſion one or more Conſtables to be appointed for the fiſhing Iſlands, and Indyans to have equall Juſtice and Dispatch.

The Duke's ſloop now ſent in the King's ſervice to remaine there all winter, to be conſtantly employed on the coaſt as occaſion, and to take and make prizes, and bring to the Commander in the Fort, any ſhall bee found on the coaſt contrary to the above orders, and the Commander to ſecure or ſend the ſame to Yorke as occaſion, and to take like care thatt the orders and regulations be punctually obſerved neare and under command of the Fort, or tranſgreſſors duly puniſh't.

The Commander if conveniency, and deſired, to receive and ſecure in the Fort the traders beſt Goods or Effects, to which they may reſort att fitting times, and have them when occaſion.

Any Trader or other truſting an Indyan or Indyans except for dry proviſſions, or adulterating Rumme or ſtrong drinke by mixing water or otherwiſe, to forfet the ſame to the party truſted or buying, and be lyable to further cenſure as the Case may require and the forfieture of the remaining part of ſuch ſtrong Liquor to bee to the Commander, ſatisfying or paying the informer.

The Indyans if plancks att hand or when had, to have an Indyan houſe made over the water, where they may reſort and bee.

New-Yorke, September the 22th 1677.
The above by unanimous advice of my Councell to bee punctually obſerved.

E. ANDROSS.

[New-York Colonial MSS. xxvii.]

At a Councell held in New-Yorke the 20th day of Apr Anno Domini 1678.

Upon the addreſſe & Requeſt of Mr William Bowditch of Salem in New England Merch.t ſetting forth his having purchaſed two Ketches from their Owners, the which were brought into Pemaquid by the Indyans upon the Agreement of Peace made the latter end of the Sum̃er, & hee deſiring an order for their delivering unto him tendring ſecurity to pay ſalvage or other Charges they may be lyable unto.

The ſame being taken into Conſideracõn, together with the great damage the ſaid Ketches are like to ſuſtaine by lyeing longer in the condicõn they are,

Ordered That they bee delivered unto the ſaid Mr Bowditch or whom he ſhall appoint to receive them together with their Appurtenances hee giving ſecurity here, to pay or make good what ſalvage, or other charges the ſaid Ketch ſhall bee Lyable to & adjuſted to pay by the Go: at his Returne. The which Capt Cæſar Knapſon the Com̃ander at Fort Charles is hereby deſired forthwith to give order & cauſe to bee done

By order of the Councell.

Letter from Lieut Gov. Brockholls to Capt Knapton

[New-York Colonial MSS. xxvii.]

N. Yorke. June 7. 1678

CAPT. KNAPTON.

Sr. Yors of the 23d of the laſt month came to my hands the begining of this weeke at the arrivall of Hermanus Sloope who brought Corp^{ll} Caren Tho: Mathews and C Roades with him: I am ſorry for the misfortune of the former The D^{rs} extraordinary care of him deſerves a Requital Matthews I ſoon com̃itted to the hole in the Fort, (who had rec^{d} his merritt if you had im̃ediately run him through upon the affront given you) & Roades hath taken Poſſeſſion of the State houſe whoſe Inſolence & Impudence is beyond compare hee ſtanding ſtill in his Juſtificacõn, though hee hath very little to ſhew for him ſelfe to beare him out, If hee were at Boſton probably they would truſſe him up, but I thinke it will bee beſt to keepe both the one & the other in durance untill the Go: returne (which wee daily expect,) when they may bee made Examples: I hope hee will approve of what wee haue done in ordering the delivery of the Ketches to Mr Bowditch upon ſecurity, however wee think wee haue done for the beſt, & that without any ſiniſter end.

The newes hee brought you of lett^{rs} from the Go: & a Packet in Mr Taylers hands for New Yorke was very true, & it arrived here from thence in little time, by Tho: Lewis ſloope who was then there & ready to come away:

The Go: Letters were dated ffeb. 10.th The ſhip he went in gott, in 23 dayes, to the ſoundings off the lands end where the wind proving contrary, they put in to Ireland from thence went to Milford Haven in Wales ſo over land to London where they arrived the 5th of January,

There were great Rumo.[rs] & preparacõns for a warre with France, The K propoſing to ye Parliam.[t] to have a ſupply for the maintenance of ninty Capitall Shipps, & thirty or forty thouſand ſoldyers.

The Go: was knighted & diſpatch't away for Guernſey, there to make but little ſtay to returne in order to his cōming back hither but when hee writte hee had effected nothing of the buſineſſe hee went about. in Eng[l] ſo knew not what delayes hee may haue mett with ſince. There was little more of Newes he writte about. Wee have not yet any certaine newes of the warre being broken out, though more than propable it is, yet Letters from Engl of Mar: 26. ſay no warre then. As for a ſupply of men you mention in lieu of thofe that are dead & that you now fend, Truly wee are not in a condicõn to doe it but expect the Go: will bring recruites both for yo[u] & us too, as wee fhall bee ill provided ag[st] an Enemy wee have fitted up the Fort pretty well, with new platt-formes & carriages, wch were much out of repaire. The Mayo[r] & Aldermen are employing their Companyes of the train band about their Fortifications:

The Agreement of Peace made by the Gents of Pifcataway & the Indyan Sachems, between them & the weft fide of Kinnebeck River I think is a good piece of worke, for that it will remove the apprehenfions you had of them before:

The Articles you fent, as alfo the examinacõns and other papers about Roades & Alden, I fhall referve for y[e] Go:

It feemes the Pinnace had better keep there; the f[d] floope that was out a Cruifing & Lieut Sharpe did well in bringing the Ketch & Roades into Pemaquid, their trading there being expreffe ag.[st] the Go: orders: The matter is well knowne here having loft a good Ketch formerly to the Dutch & had this given him in Exchange (as I am informed) when hee comes, wee ſhall heare what hee will ſay in his Juſtificacõn, but I admire hee ſhould run ſuch a hazard & ſuffer himſelfe to bee deceived by ſuch an Impoſto[r] as Roads: hee himſelfe being likewiſe a Mem[b] where Roads was condemned to bee hanged for Piracy, ſo that I thinke hee will have but little thankes from the brethren, to joyne intereſt with ſuch a cheate.

It was kindly done of Madackowando to give you the notice of their . . . . . . a trading:

As for M[r] Sturts Informacõn hee did neither wiſely nor civilly in it, however the matter being paſt & hee expreſſing his being troubled for it, I ſhall paſſe it by without ſaying more of it, but hee may bee adviſed for the future not ſo buſily to intermedle in other peoples buſineſs.

Thus having as neare as may bee anſwered the particulars of yo[r] letter, I remaine S[r]

Yo[r] humble Servant

N. Y. June 7.th 1678.

Order for the ſurrender of a Ketch.

[New-York Colonial MSS. xxvii.]

At a Councell &c June: 12. 1678

Pres^{t}.

The Councell

Mr May . . .

& Delavall.

The occaſion of meeting was the Arrivall of Mr John Alden of Boſton, whoſe caſe & Examinacõn had beene returned here before the Cōmander from Pemaquid, His Ketch[1] having beene ſeized upon in St Georges River to the Eaſtward, by order of the ſ^{d} Cōmander for trading in thoſe parts with the Indyans or others, contrary to the order of this Governm^{t}; & ſhee lyeing thereupon under arreſt together with her cargoe at Pemaquid,

Whereunto the ſ^{d} Mr Alden pleading Ignorance of the ſ^{d} order, & beleiving not to have infringed the ſame ſuppoſing thoſe parts where hee had traded & then was in, were without the bounds of his R: H^{s}. patent, & within the conqueſt made by

[1] From a rough draft of theſe minutes, with that from which this was copied, it appears that this veſſel was named the Guift, of Boſton.

the duke upon the French in thoſe parts, in the yeare 1674. As hee was informed by John Roades, who hee had hired to bee with him as being knowne in thoſe parts & acquainted with the trade and was one of thoſe that accompanyed the Duke privateer in that Expedicōn, The ſ[d] M[r] Alden likewiſe repreſenting the great loſſe hee had formerly ſuſteyned in the late Dutch warre together w[th] his great charge at home & innocence farre from preſumption in y[t] he had acted, Therefore deſiring the favo[r] of the Councell that hee might haue his Ketch & Cargoe reſtored unto him:

Upon Conſideracōn had of the Caſe & the good character of the p[r]ty it is ordered, That the ſ[d] Ketch & Cargoe now under arreſt at Pemaquid as aforeſ[d] bee delivered back to the ſ[d] John Alden or his order (the which C. Caeſar Knapton Cōmander of ffort Charles in Pemaquid is deſired to ſee done upon receit hereof) Hee the ſ[d] John Alden having given ſecurity of 240[lb] for the paym[t] of 120[lb] here if at the Go: returne ſhee ſhall be Condemned a Prize for breach of the Order afoer mencōned: the ſ^d ſume of 120^lb being by Merch^ts adjudged to bee the value of the ſ^d Ketch & Cargoe.

By Order of the Councell

Letter from Lt Gov Brockhols to C Knapton

July 1st 1678.

[New-York Colonial MSS. xxvii.]

Having rec^d a letter from Capt. Saliſbury of the 24th paſt, concerning ſome preparacōns & intended deſignes of the Maques ag^st their Ennemyes, I was willing to advertize you of it, by this opportunity of Gabriell Thompſons goeing to Boſton, (who hath promiſt to take care of the conveyance of this to you.)

I the rather give you this intelligence being informed that the Vnnagoungos are the Indyans neare yor parts, which if ſo, probably yor giving them notice to bee upon their Guards, will lay ſome obligacōn of friendſhip upon them, the which you may advize with Mr Jocelyn about and accordidgly act therein:

Wee are all well here, but no farther newes from the Go: yet, nor of any certa'ty of Peace or Warre. Having nothing more to comunicate I take leaue & remaine,

S[r] Yo[r] friend & Serv[t].

A Copie of that pt of Co Salisburyes lett[r] relating thereunto I have sent here inclosed . . . . . the rather &c.

My Service to Mr Jocelyn.
... Nicolls desires his may bee } July 1st 1678:
... resented to y[e] both.

Council Orders relating to Pemaquid.

[Council Minutes vol iii. Part II. Page 180.]

At a Councell held in New Yorke August the 23[d] 1678.

The Affaires of Pemaquid being taken into consideracon — Resolved That the former orders sent there relating either to Christian or Indyan doe continue in force untill the Spring, as farre westward as Blacke Point when his Hon[r] the Governour to goe there and take order about the Settlem[t] of Planters or Inhabit[ts] trade and all other matters of which notice is to bee given or in the meane time, any others may apply as occasion at New Yorke.

That no Indyan Trade bee admitted at Pemaquid but from and to this place to prevent Inconvenience.

That the Garrison Officers and Souldy.rs doe continue in ye ffort there untill the Spring Except Sicke or unfitt persons desiring it, shall have Leave to Come away.

* * *

A Speciall Commission to the Court of Sessions att Pemaquid for the Tryall of Isreal Dymond and John Rashly About the Drowneing of Sam.ll Collins.

[Orders Warrants &c xxxii½.]

Sr Edmund Andros.

Kn.t &c. To Ensigne Thomas Sharpe Commander att Pemaquid John Joslyne Esqr Justice of the peace in Quorum, Mr John Dollin Mr Lawrance Dennis and Mr. John Jourdaine Justices of the Peace Greeting Whereas upon Informacōn that Israel Dymont and John Rashly Stand

Committed about the Drowneing of Samuel Collins from on board the Ketch Cumberland Whereof the ſaid Dymont was Maſter in yor parts, To the end that they may be braught to their faire and Legall Tryall and Juſtice Duly Adminiſtered, I doe hereby Appoint Authorize and Impower you at yor next or vſuall Court of Seſſions to be holden att Pemaquid aforeſaid to Call before you the Perſons of the ſaid Iſrael Dymont and John Raſhly and them upon Such Indictm^{t} p^{r}ſenm^{t}, or Complaint, that ſhall be Exhibited on ſaid matter to heare try and Examine, and ſuch Judgm^{t}, or Sentance to pronounce and Declare thereupon as the Law in Such Caſes Directs, and to cauſe the ſame to be Duly Executed accordingly And for ſoe Doeing this ſhall be yor ſufficient warr^{tt} and Diſcharge. Given under my hand and Sealed wth the Seale of the Prouince &c Dated the 6:th of January: 1680.

Council Orders relating to Pemaquid.

[New-York Colonial MSS. xxix.]

At a Councell &c. June 24th, 1680.

Ordered, That ſome perſons bee appointed to goe from hence to Pemaquid, for holding Co^{rts}.

That in their way they call in at ffiſhers Iſland, the Governm^{t} whereof is to bee aſſerted, & that a Conſtable bee appointed there. They are likewiſe to put in at Martins Vineyard & Nantucket, that fitt Magiſtrates may be elected & confirmed there & that they be required to ſend one of their former number hither, to anſwer their neglect in not making due returnes of their Elections the laſt Yeare.

Blanck Civill Com̃iſſions for Martins Vineyard & Nantuckett.

Military Com̃iſſions for Pemaquid.

June 26. Saggadock magiſtrates or offic^{rs} to continue, the Co^{rt} to try onely for 40^{s} inſtead of 5^{lb} formerly granted them.

ffiſhermen to come to Pemaquid yearly to renew their Engagen^{ts}, & not to ſplitt or fling out their Gurry, or to trade with the Indyans to the prejudice of the fiſhery & hazard of thoſe parts

Capt Knapton & M[r] Weſt to haue comiſſion to joine with the Co[rt] there.

Land to bee given out indifferently to thoſe that ſhall come & ſettle, but no trade to bee at any other place than Pemaquid & none at all with the Indyans as formerly ordered.

The Juſtice alone or any two of the Commiſſion[rs] or Aſſiſtants to haue permiſſion (out of Co[rt]) to judge of any caſe or treſpaſſe under the ſume of 40[s].

At a Councell &c June 25, 1680.

Preſent the Gov & Councell.[1]

* * * *

Pemaquid.

C. Knapton, to goe to Pemaquid

The Go[rs] ſpeech to the Indyans when there.

M[r] Jocelyn a comiſſion to bee Juſtice

[1] From a rough draft full of eraſures and interlineations.

Mr Potter Laurence Durrie, & Richard Redding to be Comiſſionrs & Aſſiſtts in the Corts of ſeſſions, to try to 20lb .... Cort.

A Comiſſion for the Juſtices &c.

Appeal to the Aſſize

Sagadock Magiſtrates are... to continue the Cort to try only for 40s in ſtead of 5lb formerly granted them.

Land to be given out indifferently to thoſe that ſhall ſettle but no trade but at Pemaquid & none at all with the Indyans as formerly ordered.

All ffiſhermen to come to Pemaquid yearly to renew their engagemt. and not to ſplitt or fling out their Gurry on ye fiſhing ground or to trade with the Indyans to the prejudice of the fiſhery & hazard thoſe pts.

C. Knapton & Mr Weſt to haue comiſōns to joyne with the Cort there.

The Juſtice alone or any 2, comiſſionrs to have power to judge of any caſe under 40s

* * * * *

A Commission to Capt. Caesar Knapton and Mr John West to bee Justices att Pemaquid.

[General Entries xxxii. 92.]

Sr Edmund Andros Knt. &c By vertue of his Maties. Letters pattents and the Commission and Authority unto mee given under his Royall Highnesse I doe hereby in his Maties. name Constitute & Appoint you Capt Cæsar Knapton and Mr John West to bee Justices of the peace at Pemaquid and dependences Giving you full power & Authority to act as Justices of the peace according to Law, and former practice; And all persons whom it may concerne are Strictly Charged and Required to give you due Respect and obedience accordingly Given under my hand and seale of ye Province this 26th day of June in the 32th yeare of his Maties Raigne Annoq Dominj 1680

A Commission for Henry Joceline Esqr to bee a Justice of the Peace in Quorum &c to bee Justices at Pemaquid.

Sr Edmund Andros Knt. &c By vertue of his Maties. Letters Pattents and the Commiſſion and Authority unto mee given under his Royall Highneſſe I doe hereby in his Maties name Conſtitute and Appoint you Henry Joceline, Eſq^{r} to bee Juſtice of the Peace in Corum and you Mr John Dollen Mr Laurence Dennis Mr Richard Redding & Cõmander of Pen to bee Juſtices of the peace together with the Cõmander of Pemaquid for the time being to bee a Court of Seſſions to bee held in Pemaquid for the Jurisdiccõn thereof Giving you or any of you (whereof the Juſtice of the peace in Corum or Cõmander to bee one) full power and Authority to keepe a Court and to act according to Law and former practiſe, And all perſons whom it may concerne are ſtrictly Charged and Required to give you due reſpect and obedience accordingly This Commiſſion to bee of force for the ſpace of one whole yeare from the date hereof and till renewed Given under my hand and Seale of the Province in New Yorke this 26th day of June in the 32th yeare of his Maties Raigne Anno q Dominj 1680.

Council Orders relating to Pemaquid.

[New-York Colonial MSS. xxix.]

N. Y. At a Councell &c Sept 14, 1680.

Pres^{t} The Go: & Councell--&c

C Knapton
M^{r} Weſt.

Pemaquid affaires by C Knapton & M^{r} Weſt

Izrael Dymont & John Raſhly; questioned at y^{e} .... orders there held 4th Aug. laſt--for drowning Sam Collins & being aboue their Cogniſance &c referred to Next Co^{rt} in Pem & ordered to have a Com̃iſſion ſent there to this purpoſe.

Walter Moore &c .....

Henry Palmer--Dep^{t}--for Debt

An order of Co^{rt} ſerved

The Co^{rt} to bee the laſt Wedneſday in June & firſt in No^{r}. The next Co^{rt} in June.

Severall ord^{rs} paſt read, ſigned by M^{r} Weſt Clarke. & Lre to Juſtice Jordan &c

To write to Pemaquid that what is done is approved of & about the Maques that they are forbid, & that they ſhould do the like by their Indyans, not to goe out one ag^{ſt} ye other to warre

A Letter to Enſigne Sharpe att Pemaquid

[Orders Warrants &c xxxii½.]

Septembr ye 15th 1680.

Enſigne Sharpe

Yours by Capt. Knapton received I have ſent you by this bearer thirty pounds in mony which I would haue you with the advice of Capt Redding Lay out on a good Sailing Shallop.

That may be for the forte or Publikue Vſe theire but Suppoſe you may light on one Cheaper. I heare things at preſſent are well and in good Ordr and hope you will ſo Continue Take Care to keepe the plattforme in the fort in good repaire wch I judge you may doe by Wattering or throwing ſtuffe or Earth thereupon Prſuming that noe ordinary weight Cann Prjudice it I haue alſoe ſent you ſupplyes * * * for as pr incloſſed Invoice, And am

Yor Affectionate friend

E. A.

A Letter to Mr Justice Jordaine att Richmond Island nere Caskobay.

[Orders Warrants &c xxxii½.]

New Yorke the 15th of Septembr 1680

Mr Justice Jourdaine,

Capt Knapton and Mr West being arrived have Given me an account of their actings Eastward and yor particuler well faire which I shall alwayes Endeavour, and to that end doubt not of your redynesse to performe and execute the trust in you reposed as Settled not apprehending any alteracōn or inovacōn of Governmt. butt may assure yorselfe that each person in Authority discharging their duty shall have all Just protection and Encouragmt, and be Endemnified accordingly I have taken care to prevent Mahakes incussons by forwarning said Mahakes warring with our Indyans and now send like ordrs for or said Indyans wch I doubt not will be observed however aught not to bee Carelesse I shall not bee wanting in my duty in Every respect and as occasion lett you heare from me of which you are not to faile on your parts and wth Commendations to others authorized in your parts wth you Remaine:

Your Affectionate friend
E. A.

Order for restraining Indian Hostilities.

[Orderr Warrants &c xxxii½.]

The Governo^rs ord^r to be Declared to the Indyans att Pemaquid sent to the Commander and Magistrates there

The Governo.^r hath sent to forbid the Mahakes and doth lett you know you must not warr upon each other being within and of the Governm^t. But whereas many partyes may be out you will doe well Carefully to looke out and avoyd all surprises till you be Assertained all are returned home and things Quiett and Well. The Cheifest Sachems to be sent for and the aboue ord^r Signified to them after wch to give then Something more then they could Deserve for Comeing such a Journey.

Sep^tb: ye 15th 1680.
E A.

A Letter to Ensigne Sharpe.

[Orders Warrants &c xxxii½.]

New Yorke ye 15th. Septembr 1680.

Ensigne Sharpe.

I have by Mr Wells and one writt by Mr West answered yours of the 7th Instant except what relates to Mr Joslyne whom I would have you use with all fitting respect Considering what he hath been and his age, And if he Desire and shall build a house for himselfe to lett him Choose any lott and pay him ten pound towards it or if he shall Desire to hyre soe to live by him selfe then to Engage and pay the rent either of which shall be allowed you in yor account as alsoe sufficient provision for himselfe and wife as he shall Desire out of the Stores letting me know pr this returne how hee desires it or what, that I may Settle it. Commendations to Mrs Sharpe

I remaine,
Yor. Affectionate friend
E. A.

A Commiſſion for Capt ffrancis Skinner to be Commandr att Pemaquid and Parts Eaſtward.·.

[Orders Warrants &c. xxxii½.]

By the Com̄ander in Chiefe

I doe hereby Conſtitute and appoint you Capt ffrancis Skinner to be Commandr att Pemaquid and Parts Eaſtward under the Governmt. of his Royll. Highneſſe you are therefore to take Care that the Militia in the ſeverall Places be well armed Duly Exerciſed and Kept in good ordr. and Diſcipline and the officers and ſouldrs thereof are Required to obey you as their Commandr, and yorſelfe to obſerve ſuch ordrs and Direccōns as you ſhall from time to time Receive from me or other yor ſuperiour Officers according to the Rules and Diſcipline of Warr and the truſt Repoſed you Given undr my hand and Seale in New Yorke this 30th of Auguſt 1681.

A. B.

Instructions for Capt Ffrancis Skinner Commander att Pemaquid.

[Orders Warrants &c. xxxii½.]

Att yor Arrivall att Pemaquid you are to Demand of the Present Command.^r and take possession of the Garrison or fforte there and to take into yor. Charge Care and Management the Sould^rs there-unto Belonging and for them to Provide and furnish all Due Provisions and necesaryes as formerly.

You are Likewise to take an Exact account of all Stores and Ammunition as you shall find there and send me an account thereof and what Condicōn you finde the place in and of yor voyage thither.

You are to be verry Carefull to Prevent any Disorders or Trouble amongst Indians and others and to see that they be Civilly vsed as formerly and that the ord^rs about Regulateing the trade and ffishery be observed.·.

You are to keep Due account of all Disbursm^ts for the fforte or Souldiers or othear publique Charge, and send the same to me with an account of yor Proceedings and actings from time to time by all Convenient Oppertunity

Given und[r] my hand in New Yorke the 30th Day of August 1681.

A B.

Letter from Lieut Gov. Brockholls to Ensign Sharpe.

[Orders Warrants &c xxxii½.]

New Yorke Aug[st]: the 30[th] 1681.

Ensigne Thom. Sharpe.

I have herewith for yo[r] Reliefe sent Capt[t]: Skinner to be Command[r] for Pemaquid and Parts Eastward You are therefore to Deliver up the Garrison and Sould[r]s now und[r] yo[r] Command to him and by the first Oppertunity Repaire heither which will be necessary as soone as possible M[r] Wells Being Goeing for England that you settle yo[r] accounts with him before his Departure.

Remaine

Yo: Affectionate ffriend

A: B:

Extract from a letter of Lieut Gov. Brockholls, to the Governor, dated New York Sept: 17th, 1681.

[Orders Warrants &c xxxii½.]

* * * *

What men are Left I Continue att Pemaquid Severall Being Deaed and Apprehensions of Trouble wth the Indians. Cannot more Lessen the Garrison there, But haue sent to Releiue Sharpe that he may make up his accounts with Mr Wells Before his Departure for England which is Intended with my Lady in the Beaver who Judge will be Ready to Saile about a month this time.

* * * *

Articles of Association for the Settlement of a town upon Sheepscot River.

[New-York Colonial MSS. xxxiv.]

Att a Meeting att Mr Robert Gibbers House att ffort hill in Boston Held this nintenth Day of Augst in ye thirty fourth yeare of ye Reigne of our Souerigne Lord Charles ye Second by ye grace of God of

England Scotland ffrance and Ireland King, Defender of ye ffaith: & Annoq Chrifty: 1682 Wittneffeth; That whereas there was a neck of Land Suruaide & a towne Laid out vpon ye Said necke Generally knowne & called by ye name of Mafons & Jewtts neck Lieing & beeing in Shipscutte Riuer,& a towneſhip bounded to y^e ſaid towne; ye ffourth Day of July Extent by Sq^e Joſlinge Juſtis In Corrum with ſeurall other of ye fformer Inhabitance of ſaid Riuer in Company with y^e ſaid Juſtis as Afforeſaid; therefore it was thought neſſicary & Conuacniant ffor ye proppigatting & Bennifitt of Said towne & towneſhipe & ffor ye privilidges theirof to call this Meeting where was Mett ſeuerall of ye fformer proprieto^rs: & Inhabitance with their Aſſociats whoſe names are vnderneath Subſcribed who Did Joyntly Bind themſelues to ſtand to seuerall Articles of Agreement ffor y^e ſettelling and Sittuating of ſaid towne & towneſhipe for ye good & Benniſiſhall Aduancement theirof; theirfor to that purpoſe this Couenant & Agreement is Drawne; & is Affearmed with ye hand

& ſeale of Euery perſon heare p[r]eſent y[e] Artickles ffolloweth, Viz.

Imp[r]s. Firſt. Itts: thought neſſicery that Euery fforemer Inhabitante properiato[r] & owne[r] of any Lands Medow grounde & ſalt or ffreſh with all their fformer priuilidges wrights or tittalles in any wiſe whatsoeuer of their former Rights Into y[e] fforeſaid towneſhipe ffor y[e] ffuter good & bennifitt theirof muſt & ſhall bee throwne Into ſaid towneſhipe y[e] ffruitt trees barnes houſing & ffencing ſtuff only to bee Excepted but all other priuilidges of any perſon or perſons whatsoeuer muſt & ſhall belonge to ſaid towneſhip as aboue is ſpeſified.

Secondly. Itts ffurther Agreed that Euery perſon & perſones whatsoeuer that Intend, to Settell build plant & Mannuer in y[e] ſaid towne thus Laid out & Suruayed ffor that Intent muſt & ſhall Repaire to y[e] ſaid neck of Land or towne as affore menſhoned: to make preperration ffor their ſettelling & building of ſaid towne twelue mounths Affter the twenty ninth Day of September Inſuing y[e] Date of theſe p[r]eſents in y[e] yeare 1683; y[e] 29: Day of

September beeing ye ffirthest tim Appoynted According to Agreement vpon ye fforfituer & penelty of Lousing all their wrights & tittells to or of any part or parsell of said towne or towneshipe Except such properiaters Children that are att prentis or not att agg^{e}: then to Mannuer & possess their Lotts: when Layd out p^{r} Men which must & shall bee Chosen p^{r} y^{e}: Towne ffor that Intent & purpose.

Thirdly. Itts ffurther Agreed that their shall bee a speshall & speedy order taken that their may bee a Conueniante place as a tract of Land Laid out for A Ministree with a Conueniant place to sett a meeting house to ye best aduantage for ye towne & allso that wee may haue a minister of our owne ffree choyce & such a man as ye Mager parte of ye towne shall Like & Approue of ffor that End.

ffourthly, Itts ffurther Concluded that as sone as any Men that haue subscribed their hands & seales to these p^{r}esents shall or may come to Make way ffor bulding or settelling they may & shall haue ffree Leaue & Lycence to Lay out & bound their home Deuiſhones that Lyes near yᵉ towne without Any hendrance or Diſturbance of or by any perſon or perſons whatſoever; moreouer it is Agreed that noe perſon nor perſons whatſoeuer ſhall buld any veſells ſmall or great Cutt or Cary away any timber ſpeares ffencing ſtuffe hay thache or any other Marchendyes out of ſaid towne or townſhipe without yᵉ Leaue Licence & Approbaccõn of ſaid towne Inhabitance then & their ſettelled.

ffifthly. Itts Likewiſe Agreed that all ſuch perſones that ſhall or may firſt ſettell & are their Reddy to Improue their lotts as ffencing & working ffor yᵉ Improuements of Said home Lotts Shall & may haue free Liberty & Licence to Lay out & bound their out Deuiſhons for their beter Aduantage & fforwarding of their Improuements without any hendrance or Diſturbance of any perſon or perſones whatſoever & Euery mans Lotts ſhall be Equally Deuided euery manes equall proportion of Vplands & meadow both freſh & ſalt with all other..... toune ſhall ſee it........ ffor yᵉ ſaid towne ....

Sixtly. Itts ffurther Agreed that euery man both houſe keepers & ſingell perſones att y[e] Agge of ſixtene yeares; muſt & ſhall prouide three pounds of good powder with twelve pounds of Lead bullet & Swann ſhot: ffor a towne Store & allſo to keep a good ffier Loke muſcet or ffowling gonne all to bee Redy for a ſtoke to preuent y[e] heathen or a forrin Inuaſhon: & to haue two Sufficient men Choſen for that end to ſee euery man ſo provided according to order.

Seuenthly. Itts Likewiſe ffirther Agreed: that noe perſon nor perſones muſt not neither ſhall they nor any of them buld any dwelling houſe or Cauſe it to bee bult in Any part of y[e] towneſhipe but only vpon that neck of Land Layed out & ſuruayed for that End & purpoſe vntill ſuch time as y[e] towne ſhall ſee it meete & fitt & that it may bee ffor y[e] Aduancment & benefitt of y[e] Affore menſhoned towne & touneſhip According to Agreement.

Eightly. Itts Likewiſe ffurther Concluded that Euery Inhabitant of ſaid

Towne & towneſhip muſt & ſhall haue free Liberty & Licence without any Diſturbance or Moleſtation of any perſon or perſones whatſoever to tranſport any timber planke ſpeares pip ſtaues or any other prouiſhon or Marchandize whatſoeuer with any veſell or veſells great or ſmall to any porte or ports that are ffree as Boſton or Els where without paying any Dutyes or Cuſtomes in Eſpeſhall maner ye grauth of our owne Country; where wee Inhabit.

Ninthly. Itts moreover Agreed vpon ffurther Conſiderations that Euery Anſhant & fformer properriator that haue any Children Allredy borne; that it is ffreely graunted that any of thoſe Children ſhall haue as free Liberty Leaue & Licence to Come Into ſaid towne or towneſhip of Shipscutt Riuer & haue Lotts Layd out for them by the ſelect men Choſen for that purposs of all Lands medow ground & all other priuilidges whatſoever without paying any Sumpſhan of mony or moneyes worth or any other grattuity whatſoeuer but ſhall bee as free Deniſenes as any of theſe allredy ſettelled; allſo that euery former owner Mannuerer or propriato[r] may & ſhall haue ffree Libertye Leaue & Licence to Remoue take offe or ſell all or any of their ffruit trees garden ſtuff houſing barn timber or other hewed timb[r] planke bords ffencing ſtuffe & Like except it bee y[e] timber now growing in or vpon y[e] towne or towneſhipe y[e] towne or townsmen Agreeing to this, that then y[e] ſaid Walter Phillips Jenier ſhall & will agree to & with y[e] ſaid towne & towns-men vpon all ffuter Affeares & ſtand to what they may now or hereafter Acct. in y[e] fforefittuer & penallty of Louſing all his former propriateyes within y[e] Li-mites of ſaid towneſhipe as he ſhall At-teſtie by ſubſcribing his hand to this Laſt Artickle to that end & purpoſs.

Tenthly & Laſtly. Itts moreouer Agreed that all thoſe men that haue Subſcribed their hands & ſeales to all theſe aboue Menſhoned Artickles Made y[e] 19 Day of Auguſt 1682 as aboue may & ſhall haue their ffree Liberty & Licence Ether them ore ſom of them or y[e] Mager part of them att publick Meeting Appoynted for that purpose to make Choyce of take in or Incuridge any Responsabell Credable or Benyfishall man or men of Craftsmen Merchants or ye Like without any Deniall hendrance or Molestashon: & ffor ye Manifestation & Confirmation of all & Euery of ye Aboue specified Artickles wee haue all Joyntly & seuerally hearvnto Subscribed our Hands & Seales ye Day & yeare ffirst Aboue Righten Regny Regis Carilus Secundus

As Attest. Vpon a ffurther Consideration beefore Signed & Sealed it is Intended that Euery person & persons y^t^ now doe or at any time or times heareaffter shall Manneur & Settell ye Aboue said towne & towneshipe must & shall Enioy all & euery parte & persill of said towne & towneshipe to say ye wholl Premisses & bounds thereof to bee free Lands to bee Enioyed by vs & to vs to our heires ffor Euer without any hendrance disturbance or Molestation in any wise whatsoeuer by any person or persons Except it should bee Inuaded by a forrin nashun & Deserted by all ye Inhabitance as aboue ſhall bee & now is Confirmed as p^r our hands & Seales.

W^t

JOHN ALLYEN.
THOMAS GENT.
CHRISTOPHER DYER.
THOMAS MENER
ROBERT SCOTT
his R marke
WILLIAM LOWERING
JOHN WHIT
his -I-marke.
DANIEL GENTT
his (-(marke
WILL^M WILLCUTT
JOHN BROWNE
his B. mark
JOHN DIER
his -I- marke
CALEB RAY
ELIZABETH PHYPS
hir marke
DAUID RANSFORD
his ʑ marke

Allowed by me; 30th August 1682.
HENRY TOWLYN Jus in . . .

Theſe within Articles Recorded in the Book of Records at Pemaquid and Examined by me

W^M SHORT Cl: Seſs.

We whos Names are vnder written Doe Teſtify vpon oath y^t we ſaw Henry Towlyn Eſq^r Juſtis in quo Sign this within mentioned Artickles with his own hand as wittnes our hands

WILLIAM LOUERIDGE
THOMAS GENT,
BATH ANDERSON
CHRISTO DYE Conſtable

These three men are now Sworn at New Dartmouth this 16th Day of September 1684 Before me

GILES GODDARD Just in quo

A Letter From Capt Brockholls to Justice Josline att Pemaquid, New Yorke August 24th 1682∴

[Orderr Warrants &c xxxii½.]

Sir

In Answer to yo'rs of the 17th: July I am Glad to heare of the Settlement of yor Partes which must be Encouraged and is Left to your Mannagment with the advise of the Commander and those in Place According to the Regulacōns and Orders given by the Governor, which still Remaine in Force and must be Attended and Observed accordingly The number of Persons you mencōn will add much to the strength and trade of the Country which Shall Endeavour to Supporte the Proper plans for Settlemt. You are best Acquainted with Therefore Left to you as Aforesaid to Order the Laying out what wrott by Castine is of noe Importe you Knowing the Extent of his Roy^{ll} High^{s} Limitts which must be Maintained according to his Pattent

Have nothing of news butt Dayly Expected from England all well here my Respects to yo^{u} selfe and Wife is the only needfull att p^{r}sent from

Sir

Yo^{r} Affectionate ffriend

A. B.

Commission for Settling the Duke of York's Title.

[New-York Colonial MSS. xxxiv.]

Coll Tho. Dongan Liev^{t} Govr and Vice Admirall under his Royall High^{ss} of New Yorke & Dependencyes in America.

By virtue of the authority Derived unto me I do hereby Constitute and appoint you, Ensigne Thomas Sharp John Allen Esq. Justices of the peace Mr Richard Pattishall Mr Alex^{r} Waldrop Mr Thomas

Gyles or any three of you to be Commissioners for the settling his Royall Highne[s] territoryes between the River Kenebeck and S[t] Croix Giving you full power and authority to act as commissioners and to consult make rules and orders for the good and wellfare of the said places and Government and to call to question and punish all offenders according to law and practise and all persons whom it may concerne are strictly charged & required to give you due respect & obedience accordingly . . . .

Affidavits Concerning Indian Hostilities.

[New-York Colonial MSS. xxxi.]

Jan 28. 1683.

James Dennes aged 26 yeares or thare about and now liuing in Kenebeck Riuer, and Being a subject true to our Souraigne lord the King and hearing the Ingans threatning the Einglish

This deponant saith that he hard the Ingans say one that is counted a Captaine amonge them he ſaid, that his hart would neuer Be well tell he had killd ſome of the Eingliſh againe and threatening that he would Burne the Engliſh houſes and make the Engliſh Slaues to them as they ware Before. Seuerall times Before this Ingen which was called By the Engliſh Captaine Antoneie then a nother Capt ſaid to this ſaid Anthonie that he ſhould hould his peace and not tell what he had amind to doe and furder ſaid that he heard a Ingen woman ſay of her one acourd that ſhe would not Be heare when the wars was if ſhe could help it for the Ingans was ſo bad thay would make wars and ſhe could not abid to ſee her Engliſh naighbours kild and beſide ſhe was afraid the Engliſh would kill her and furder ſaith not only the Ingans are going to Canada and ſay they will be Back againe in apreill inſuing the Date here of

Giuen on oath before me

LAURENCE DENNY
Juſtes of Peaſe

Date ffebury 22. 1683.

John Hornibroke aged 30 yeres or thare about.

This deponant ſaith that it is a genurall ſaing among the Ingens that they will haue wars againe and furder ſaith that thare was four Ingans lay at his houſe and one of the Ingans ſaid that he would Stab a Engliſh man with his knive and Run away when he had dun and furder ſaith that a Ingan ſaid that the hachet hung ouer our heads and he did not know how ſonne it might fall and Before that was he would giue John Hornibroke notice that he might go away and he was a weary of keeping the Ingans for falling out with the Engliſh and he would keep them no longer and furder ſaith that the Ingans did threaten to burne Engliſh houſes and make them Slaues as they ware Before and furder ſaith

As farr as I vnderſtand by John Hornibroke that the aboue ſaid writing is Reported by the Indians for truth JOHN ROWDON

That the Ingans did Report that they would go to Canada and fetch ſtrength to fall on the Engliſh and ſome of the Chefe of them is gon to Canada all Ready to fetch guns and amanition and they ſaid that they would make the greateſt armie that euer yet among them.

LAURENCE DENNY
Juſtes of the peace

The Depoſhiſhon of John Voanny & Will Bacon ye one Agged 55 yeares & ye other 35 Dito

Teſtifieth & Saith,

That y^e^ ſaid partyes ſetting fforth one purpoſe in ye beehalfe of ye Reſt of ther neghbors & with their vrgent Requeſt & Deſier to ſearch out ye truth of ye Ingen newes y^t^ was going Amongſt vs. Wee did take our Viage ffrom Kenybecke to Caſco bay wheare wee did Repeare to Mr James Andrews houſe to learn how Affears went their & y^e^ ſaid Andrews did willingly Informe vs that ane Indion which did Comenly Repear to his houſe & Mr Walter Cendalles ffor Releefe did ſay if y^e ſaid Andrews & Cendall would not diſcloſe his name that then hee would diſcloſe what hee knew Conſerning ye Indons Againſt ye Engliſh & Affter thay had promiſed hee told them that ye Indones was Minded to Riſe in Rebellyon againe & Cutt off ye Engliſh but how ſone hee could not yett tell but when thay did & hee ſee their Reſalution hee would ſend them or bring them a burch Rine as though hee had brought them a Leter & ffurther ſaith not

Y^e ſame deponent further ſaith y^t .... did Informe them that thay had ffallen one a ffortnight agone had thay not disagreed in their Judgment which did all that time preuent their Abſolute Intenſhons & further ſaith not

Tacken before me this
28 day of ffebruary 1683

P^r JNO ALLYEN Jus of Peace

The Depoſhiſhon of John Molton Aged 50 yeares or their abouts tes-tyfieth & Saith,

That hee being Cutting of wood in his ffeld y^{t} goodwife Cutery called to him & ſaid that ſhould luke to himſelfe for their was an Indeon would do him a miſchiefe & y^{e} ſaid Molton Luked about & ſaw an Indeon Coming threw ſaid Cuteryes ffeild ouer to ſaid Molton without ſpeaking one word but came to ſaid Molton with his knife in his hand and profered to ſtab ſ^{d} John Molton wth y^{e} ſame twice, & then ſaid Molton defended himſelfe with his Axe & threatining y^{e} ſaid Indon to Cut out his braynes with y^{e} Same & when y^{e} ſaid Indeion ſee that, hee Deperted ffrom y^{e} ſaid John Molton & went towards Mr Samuell Boles his houſe & ffurther ſaith not.

Taken upon oath before mee
ffebuary y^{e} 28 Day 168$\frac{3}{4}$

Pr Jno Allyene Jus of Peaſe

A Letter from Capt Brockholls to Mr Ffrancis Skinner att Pemaquid

[General Entries xxxiii. 55.]

New Yorke May 10th: 1683.

Mr Ffrancis Skinner

Sr

Am Sorry the Loosnesse and Carelessenesse of your Command gives Oppertunity for Strangers to take notice of your Extravigancyes and Debaucheryes and that Complaints must come to me thereof being what your Office and Place ought to prevent and punish, to which perceive have Little Regard nor to the former Orders and Regulacōns for Settlement being alsoe Informed that you have Suffered People to settle alone in Remote Places Contrary thereto Exposeing themselves to the fury of the Heathen which may Proue of ill Consequence as hath been allready Experience to all in those Partes, Expect a better observance and Comporte for the future, and that Sweareing Drinking and Prophanesse to much practiced & Suffered with you will be wholly Suppressed and that you haue Due

Regard to all former Orders and Regulacõns for Settlement &c by Mr Pattishall Shortly Intended your way I shall Send Commission for another in the Place of Mr Joyslyne Deceased who feere is much wanted, I am,

Your affectionate ffriend

A. B:

A Letter from Capt Brockholls to Justice Lawrence Dennis &c

[General Entries xxxiii. 56.]

New Yorke May 10th 1683:

Mr Lawrence Dennis.

Sir.

Yours of the ninth of Aprill Received by which am troubled to heare Such Loosenesse and Extravigancy att Pemmaquid and Remissenesse in the Officer or Commander there not to observe the former Orders and Regulacõns for Settlements being noe wayes altered but Continued & Confirmed All Care possible hath been and is taken of that parte of the Governmt by Giving Good and necesſary Orders which You the magiſtrates and Officers muſt ſee Executed and Obſerved accordingly and Suffer none to Vylate haveing perticuler Regard to the puniſhment & Suppreſſing thoſe Debaucheryes you mencõn, about w:ch Shall Allwayes write to Pemmaquid and that none ſettle in Remote partes alone but in Townſhips according to former Orders and Regulacõns ſhall Likewiſe Commiſſionate another in the Place of Mr Joſlyne Deceſed and hope all paſte Errors will bee Rectified by your future Good Comporte the news of which will be moſt acceptable to,

Sr

Your Affectionate ffriend,

A: B:

A Commiſſion to Mr John Allen of Sheps-gutt to be Juſtice of the Peace for Pemmaquid and Dependencyes.

[General Entries xxxiii. 57.]

Anthony Brockholls Eſq^r^. Commander in Cheife and the Councell of the Province of New Yorke &c.

To Mr John Allen of Sheepgutt Greeting.

By Virtue of the Power and authority Derived unto us under his Roy^ll^ High^s^ wee Doe hereby in his Maties name Conſtitute Authorize and Appointe you Mr John Allen to be Juſtice of the Peace for Pemmaquid and Dependencyes Giveing you full Power and Authority to act as a Juſtice of the Peace according to Law and former Practice and all perſons whom it may Concerne are Strictly Charged & Required to give you Due Reſpect and Obedience accordingly. This Commiſſion to be of fforce for the Space of one whole yeare or till further Order. Given under my hand and Seale in New Yorke the 12th Day of May 1683 in the thirty fifth yeare of his Maties Reigne &c.

A: B:

Petition from the Inhabitants of Pamaquid.

[New-York Colonial MSS. xxxi.]

(Endorſed: — "A Peticõn of the Inhabitants of Pemaquid. Sept 6.th Defered untill the Govern^r go to Pemaquid; or ſend ſome body thither, only in the mean time the former orders are to be obſerved.") [1683.]

To the Right Honora^ble Coll Thomas Dongan Gouernor Generall of all his Royall High.^s Territories in America and Vice Admirall of the Seas &c and Councell.

The Humble Peticõn of the poor Inhabitants of the toune of Pemaquyd &c.

Humbly Sheweth.

That when the moſt part of the inhabitants of this place did come from New York at the ſubdueing of this Countrie here to Serue his Royall High^s; Therefor and for Seuerall other good reaſons (and Secureatie of the People) moueing your hono^r predeceſſor S^r. Edmund Andros, and Confirmed by Capt Brockholls; did giue grant and Confirme to this Toune of Pemaquid the whole trade of the Indians; directly and indirectly forbidding all other Perſons to trade with the Indians within this Collony Except at Pemaquid vnder very great Penalties as the Records here make appear. And Likewayes your hono^{r} was pleaſed in your Articles ſent by Capt Sharp to Order us here to build Laſt Spring one Blockhous at Merrimeting; which according to Order is there Ready to be raiſed; as will appear by ſome of your Peticõners who can informe ffurther; and for ſecureing Laſt Spring of his Royall High^{s} Reuenue wee ſent up one veſſell about tuenty ffour tunns well manned to trade haueing entered and paid Duties which does amount to more then all the Reſt of this Country; except Pemaquid towne as your Collectors books will make appeare. But ſince your poor peticõners Vnderſtands that Capt Sharp hath Receiued a Leter from your Hono^{r} to forbear ſetting up of the houſe vntill your Hono^{r} further advice otherwayes it could haue bin ffiniſhed.

Therfore your humble poor peticõners doth humbly beg and Deſire your hono^{r}

that our former Liberties granted to us Concerning tradeing with the Indians may be confirmed and ſtrict Charge giuen that noe other Perſon nor Inhabitant Shall trade Except they doe come and build here which will be a ſtrenghening to the garriſon of this place and for promoting his Royall High^{ss} Intereſt to Order that wee ſend up a Veſſell up Kenebeck riuer vntill your hono^{r} ſe caus to haue the blocke hous Raiſed being willing to pay Cuſtome & taxes according to orders which wee hope will be Conſiderable this fall in that Place other wayes it will be imbaſelled and wee diſabled from makeing our Liues Comfortable; Likewayes to grant your poor Peticõners an order how wee ſhall behaue towards the french in your Juriſdiction to the Eaſtw^{d} for the trade that way is Conſiderable and will promote your hono^{rs} intereſt. And your poor Peticõners ſhall euer Pray &c.

[The Signatures to the above have been cut off by ſome perſon unknown, probably for the autographs.]

Council Minutes v. 1*.

At ffort James in New Yorke September the 13th 1686. [1683.]

* * * *

Ordered that John Allen be made Sherriff of Pemaquid & Dependences, as Islands & whatever is thereto belonging, & he is to appoint the ffreeholders of Pemaquid & Dependences to meet & Chose one Representative

* * *

Commission of Thomas Sharpe as Commander at Pemaquid

[New-York Colonial MSS. xxxiv.]

By the Govern^{r}

I Do hereby constitute and appoint you Ensigne Thomas Sharp to be Commander att Pemaquid and parts Eastward vnder the Govorment of his Royall Highness you are therefore to take Care that the militia in the Severall places be well armed duly exercised and kept in good order and discipline and the officers and ſoldiers thereof are required to obey you as their Commander and yo^{r}ſelfe to obey ſuch orders and direccõns as you ſhall from time to time receive from me or other yor Superiour Officers according to the rules and discipline of warr and the truſt repoſed in You. Given under my Hand and Seale at ffort James the 10th day of Novr 1683.

Commiſſion of Alexander Woodrop as Sub-Collector and Receiver.

By the Govern^{r}

I do hereby Conſtitute and appoint you Mr Alex^{r} Woodrop to be Sub Coll^{r} and Receiver of the publiq Revenue of the Cuſtomes & Excyſe due to his Royall Highneſſe in Pemaquid and its Dependencyes on all Comoditys Cuſtomable and all liquors according to an act of the Gen^{rl} Aſſembly publiſhed the 31th day of Octo^{r} laſt of which you are to keep due account and make returnes of ſaid receipts in Specie from time to time to me or my order and all perſons concerned are required to conforme themſelves accordingly upon the penaltyes as in the ſaid act is ſpecifyed this my Comicōn to laſt only Dureing my pleaſure Given under my hand and ſeale in New Yorke the 28th day of November 1683.

Inſtructions for the Settlement of Pemaquid.

[Council Minutes v. 23.]

At a Council held at ffort James in New York November ye 22d 1683.

Prſent the Governor
Capt A Brockholls
Mr Ffr Fflypſie
I Spragge Mr Steph V Cortland
Mr Lucas Santer

The following Inſtructions & Orders were Conſidered.

Inſtructions for ye Settlement of Pemaquid

That no coaſting Veſſell ſhall trade on the Coaſt as Bumboats tradeing from Harbor to Harbor, but as ſhall Supply the Generall account for one boate or more, neither ſhall it be lawfull for him to trade in any Other Harbor, but where the boat or boats are, neither ſhall it be lawfull for him to trade with any other crew for liquors or wine Rumm, Beer Sider &c on ſuch penalty as you think fitting.

An Ordinary is to be Sett up at every Iſland or ffiſhing place by an approved man of that place

It ſhall not be Lawfull for the Ordinary keeper to ſuffer any boates crew or any men belonging to any boates Crew to ſitt & tipple to exceſſiue drinking, or unſea-ſonable houres to hinder the ſaid boates Crew upon ſuch penalty as by you ſhall be thought fitte

It ſhall not be lawfull for any maſters of veſſells to ſell or diſpoſe of to any Crew beſides their own any liquor of what kind ſoever on penalty or forfeiture to make good to the Veſſels Crew the ſame

It ſhall not be lawfull that after any Crew be Ship'd & agreed to proceed on their Voyage & haue been to ſea together to make a faire that if at any time by any of the Crews obſtinacy or Idleness or any other means (ſickneſſe only ex-cepted) that the Crew be ſo hindered of makeing her faire the penalty & forfeiture for each faire be confidered & fo proportionable for a longer time that the Said party fhall abfent himfelf to the Hinderance of the Veffell going to fea.

It fhall not be Lawfull for any Veffells Crew that belongeth not to the Government to make a Voyage in the Goverment, except he hath an houfe & ftaye within the Goverment on penalty of forfeiture of paying for makeing his voyage

It fhall not be lawfull for any Veffell or Veffells that do not belong to this Goverm[t] to make an herring Voyage at Mount Niles (?) or any other place within this Government upon penalty thought fitt by you

It fhall not be lawfull for fifhermen to keep any more dogges then one to a family on fuch penalty & forfeiture as fhall be thought fitt by you

It Shall not be lawfull for the ffifhermen at Socatahock after the proclamation of this order to build any more howfes on that part of the Ifland that the Stages are of, but what they fhall be on that part to the Southward where they haue begun to build & what howses are on the Island where the stages are of must be Removed within the space of 2 years likewise all salt houses or Warehowses that Stand in the way of the flakes to be removed to a Convenient place on penalty as you think fitt

That all fishermen & planters shall be forced to haue Arms & Ammunition

That all persons whatever shall be forbidd to trade wth the Indians Saue only two howses one at Merrymeeting & the other at Pemaquid

That all Vessells out of any Goverment if they com to trade or fish shall first enter at Pemaquid or the places appointed & that they shall not goe into any other Harbour except by stress of Weather but first to Cleare & giue an Account of their design & not to break bulk before they haue so Cleared & then proceed to trade or fish as license or permitt may be granted on penalty

That no Vessell or boates Crew shall break bulk or dispose of any fish till the first of June on penalty

That the fiſhermen may haue an aſſurance of theſe plantations about Socadahock & an Incouragement therunto that the planters in Sheepſgut River & Denorall Cote & the planters in Kenebeck & New Town in particular encouraged being fit for the ffiſhermen as well as planters

That no one who takes fourſcore Acres of Land Shall haue of the ſaid Acres aboue eight Acres fronting to the Sea River or Creek & ſo proportionably for any who takes more or leſſe Ground

That no Stragling farmes ſhall be erected nor no houſes built any where under the number of twenty

The Officer who is Comãnder of Pemaquid ſhall by the advice of the Cōmrs or any two of them Seaze any Veſſell that offends contrary to the aforeſaid inſtructions & ſuch Orders as ſhall be made by you or any three of you for the well eſtabliſhing that Colony, provided allways that nothing herein ſhall be don by you repugnant & contrary to the laws of this Country, & the laws of England

And for the promoteing of piety it is requiſite that a perſon be appointed by the Comiſſioners to read prayers & the holy Scriptures

Ordered that no Veſſell or boate or Cannoe whatſoever ſhall trade nor go into any Harbo[r] or River between the Rivers Kenebeck & St Croix but what ſhall enter & Clear firſt at Pemaquid, except they are forced by ſtreſs of weather, upon forfiture of both Veſſell, & goods, & that no one whatſoever as he will anſwer it at his perill ſhall take a permitt or lycenſe to trade there from John Nellſon at Boston or any other perſon whatſoever, except ſuch as are appointed & Commisſionated by the Governor of New York

And for the further encouragement for people to go & Settle on the Dukes territories between the Kenebeck & St Croix they ſhall haue lands for themſelves & their heires without paying any Quitt-rents except a ſmall acknowledgment of one ſhilling for an Hundred Acres p[r] Ann, & that they ſhall not be lyable to be arreſted for any debts for the ſpace of ſeven Years excepting ſuch debts as they ſhall contract by occaſion of their going thither, or whilſt they inhabit on that place.

No fiſhing boats whatſoever ſhall throw over board any Garbage or Gutts or any other thing that tends to the damage of the fiſhery banks on forfeiture of their boats or Veſſells

And all Veſſells or fiſhing boates not belonging to Pemaquid or the Goverment of his Royall High^s^ are to pay as followeth

A decked Veſſell four Kentalls Merchantable fiſh & an open boate two Kentalls.

Petition from the Inhabitants of Pemaquid.

[New-York Colonial MSS. xxxii.]

To the Honred^e^ Coll Thomas Dongan Left. Gouern^r^ & Viſe Admirall vnder his Ryell Highnes of New Yorke Dependenſes in America and to his Hone^rbl^ Counſell now Sitting att New Yorke

The humble Petion of the inhabytance of the Extreme partes of his Riall Hineſs Teritory Betwene the Riuer Kenybeke and S^tt^ Croix

Humbly Sheweth

Ware as y^or^ P^e^tinor^s^ Came to vnderſtand by Seuerall Commition and in ſtrucktion ffor the Settillment of the affore ſaid partes that yor Hon^{r} Hath intended Good ffor theſe partes and all ways will wee Beliue Confferme the ſame which Giues vs Greate boulldnes to ſeeck yor Hon^{r}s protecktion and Reedres ffrom many burthen, and oppretions that are Layed vpone vs by the wonte of Lawes being Lefte to the will and pleſuer of the Millitary order by which menes the Gouerment bee Coms to vs allto Gether Arbytary which ſoe to bee is Repugnant to the Laues of England and his Maj^{eſty} Regall athority as allſo a great Reflecktion one yor Honer^{s} athority Being ffully aſhored of our Deliuerc^{e} ffrom the ſame By yor Hone.^{r} Affter ſeurill yeares ſuffring By ouer Great Diſtant ffrom New Yorke whare wee are all wayes to have oure Releefe in ſuch and the Licke Caſes =

P^{r}mis the Boody of Lawes of New Yorke and the adjaſent partes of his Ryall Hines territory hath not theſe partes in it Thare ffore humbly Requeſt that wee may bee A mimber of that Boody --

2^{ly}—Thare has ben but one . . . . . appointed ffor theſe partes which all

Caſes Com beffore and if Injuſtis Don any man vnder correcation bee it ſpoocken to the Loos of his Eſtate or Dammige to his parſon this Law Appointes noe Appeall ffor vs which priueliges is a Lowed of By yor Honr and Counſell at New Yorke and thare ffore hope yor Honer will prouide ſom way ffor ouer Releefe

3ly It hath Binne the pracktis of the Commander of Pemaquid to apprehend by fforſe of armes the kings Juſtis of the peaſe and thretten other Juſtis of the Peaſe with Putting in Irons and keping in the ffort a priſnor ſeuerall dayes with other Grand abuſſes and Villifiing Lange and ffor noe Reſon only ffollowing thare Commition Granted to the Said Juſtise of the peaſe as allſo thretnige the Deſolfing of Coarts att pleſſuer By which meanes the Kings Juſtiſes and Subjects haue bine turned bee ſides thare Buſnis: Humbly Beging Yor Honrs Releeſe in the ſame

4:thly: Whare as you Honer haue Sent formly Artickles in tittled Inſtruction ffor the ſettillment of Pemaquid which ſignyfies to yor petitioneor that yor Honrs haue thoughts of Good ffor the Inhabitance of theſe partes if a Right vnderſtanding whare as the ffurſte Inſtrucktion Declarith that noe veſſeill ſhall trad one the Coſte as bumboates ffrom Harbber to Harber but ſuch as ſhall ſupplye the Gine^{r}orall account ffor one Boate or more nether ſhall it bee Lawfull to trad in any other harber which or Inſtrucktion is much to the dammig of the in habbytance and a great Diſcorigement of others that wold Come to inhabbitte ffor anſwer to the affore ſaid Inſtruction the perſons that haue ſupplied the ffiſhery haue allways ſate ſuch Grate priſes one thare Goods that it hath ffor many Years Impoveriſhed yor poore petittiones butt of Late hath by the Reſons of Supplyes att a Cheaper Rate and not Conſarned with the Supply of boates made vs to make a more comffortable Liuing then heare to fore

Likewayes wee tacke bouldnes to accquainte yor Hono^{rs} with a Conſidderable quantidy of planters Settled and are a Coming to Settill in his Riall highnes teritory in the Eſterne partes if in corrigment ffrom Yo^{r} honer which wee Diſſpare not of Deſirring yor honer to take it into yor pieous Confideration how thefe affore faid planters fhall bee fupplyed Being abfolutly Commanded that the fupplyes fhall Difpofe of noe goods but in the harbers whare ffifhery is and to now other but the boats crue which affore faid in ftrucktion wee humbly Confeue were Given in to yor Honer by him that had to much fellfe in it and wee ffeare a Combination wth other fuppliers to the Impourifhing of Your poore petifiners as heare to ffore which in fringment of trade hath neuer Ben as wee humbly Confeue to his Majefty fubiack humbly Defiring Yo^r honer to Reliue vs in the fame---

5.th Ly Whare as the ninth Inftrucktion that the ffifher men of Sacady-hocke ILand fhall not Builde any more howefes one that parte of the Iland whare the Stages bee but fhall Remoue all thare Houfes within the Spafe of three yeares which will bee the Runing of the proprieters of ye fame but wee humbly Confeue and fartingly knowe that his Majefty by act of parlyment haue mad proclaymation that all Ilands and plafes conuenient ffor ffifhery all tho any perfon or perfons propriety fhall Bee

Improued ffor that End; as allſo S[r] Edmond Androus Conſferming of the ſame: wee ffeare yo[r] Honers in ffermation haue ben ffrom a perſon fformerly Claiming a Right thare vnto all tho pretended which parſon cane bee noe other parſon then M[r] Richard Pattiſhall which wee haue Grounds to ffeare Doth not Deſighne Good to this partes wee Humbly Requeſt yo[r] honner to Reliue yo[r] poore petyſenors in this matter.

6[th]Ly. Ware as in the thirtenth artickell that all veſſels ſhall enter at Pemaquid and att noe other place which wee humbly Conſeiue will bee Very Detrimentall to a Conſiderabell quantity of ffiſher men and planters by Reſon of the Great Distanc of Pemaquid and the Depenes and Difficulty of the bay of Pemaquid has Detained ſeuerall veſſills many Days ſom times Weeckes which has expoſed the ffiſhery and planters to Great Wontes as allſo a Great Dammige to thare Imploye ouer Humble Requeſt to Y[r] Honer is that you wold grante vs two plaſes more of Entrys and Clering the one at Nu Darthmouth in Ships Gutt riuer whare ar

Confidderable inhabbitance and meny more Coming and promſing a Conſiderable trad of ſhiping ffor maste and Lumber and all ſoe an office or ſom parſon at Sacadyhocke in Kenybec Riuer appointed ffor Entring and Clearing

7:[th]Ly Ware as the Eighteenth inſtrucktion Doth Requier noe ſettillment in thoſe partes under the number of Twenty ffamelyes which wee accknolige a very great prudence of Yo[r] Honner wee humbly Conſeue if yo[r] Honer Doth but parfer tenn ffamelyes it may much more Con Duſe to the Settelling of thoſe partes ffor tenn ffamelyes can be ffound to Settill at the ffurſte a towne ſhip when twenty Cannot be procured but when tenn ſettled ſom ſmall towne it hath all times by Expperience incurriged more to Come wee humbly Requeſt your honner to Grante the Same

8[th]ly Wee ffarther take Boulldnes to acquainte yo[r] honner of a uery Conſiderable Charge that the towne of Nu Darthmouth is Ships Gutt Riuer and Sacadyhocke in Kenybeck Riuer in Erickting of a fforte at Each place ffor Security of the in habbitance againſt the Hethin by Reſon of thretting Languge proſeding ffrom them and to bee found conſull-tation ffor ware, as allſoe thay Declaring that iff thay did not Cutt of the Engliſh now thay came to inhabitt beffore that thay wold bee to manny ffor them and to ſtrong wee humbly Requeſte yo[r] honer to prouide ſome better ſecurity ffor affter time.

all thoſe fforementioned artickells wee ar ffully parſuaded yo[r] honner has a better vnderſtanding of then wee ar Capable to infforme; not Douting as yo[r] honner has allready Deſighend Good ffor theſe partes will Grant vnto yo[r] pore petiſtnors all the affore ſaid artickells wee ſhall Euer pray

JNO ALLYEN	ELIHU GUNNISON
LARRY DENNY	CHRISTOPHER RYER
JUSTES — — — —	THOMAS GENT
NIC[H]: MANNING	WILLIAM LOWERING
THOMAS GYLES	ROBERT COOK
PHI= PARSON	FFRANCIS JOHNSONN
	AFFTE NELE
	THO SERGANT
	GOURY GRAY
	JOHN LANGE
	ELIUS TRUCKE
	JOHN SELLMAN

Richd Pateſhall Informeth Againſt Mr John Kelſon Mcht in Boſton.

[New-York Colonial MSS. xxxi.]

Saieth: yt ſome time in Deſemb:r Laſt paſt being 1683 I Ariued in Boſton & met ther with Capt Sharpe that was my paſ-enger to Rod: Iſland. I Aſked him wheth^r he was with: ye Gor Bradſtret a bout ye procleme to Aſke Leue ffor ye ſeting, of it, to yt he Anſwered noe and deſired me to goe with him, the which I did the Gouer Anſwer was ther ſhould be caer taken About it After he had met in Counſell:

I alſoe Aſked Capt Sharpe whether he had deliuered the Letter to Mr Nol . . . he ſaid noe, but would doe it After ye procla was vpp, when I vnderſtod Mr Kelſon, had his Letter I went to his houſe, to diſcorſe him Conſerneing ye Eſterne prts, wher I Aquainted him of ye Honr Gouer Dongans Reſolues to poſes him ſelfe, with his Riall Hines his Rite to St: Croys by Letters pattens Granted from his maieſt: and he had ſent Letters Accord-eing to Coſten, to Come in and pay his

Reſpect to Pemequide his Anſwer was Gou^{r} Dongan, was miſtaken in Coſten, for he was Comiſinated from ye King of Ffranſe, and Likewiſe from ye Gover^{r} of Canadey to Kepp ye Rite and poſeſion of thoſe p^{r}ts and that y^{e} ſaid Coſten was a Baron, and did Skorne to Come to Capt Sharpe being a men perſon, and of noe p^{r}ts and could not Diſcorſe ſutch a Gentell,^{m} as Coſten, further more that ye Said Coſten would Loſe, his Life Rather, and that it would be an Ill dayes workes for Gou^{r} Dongan to vſe Au:^{t} of Hoſtille^{y} towards, him, for if he did ye Engliſh in theſe p^{r}ts would ſone be Cut of, and ye plaſes Left in Aſhes. I Tould him that could not be for ye Ffrentch were but ffue, he Anſwered that theſe and all ye Indeans were Ingaged to him in theſe p^{r}ts I Anſwered that all ye Indeans from Pemiquid weſtwards waer obedient to Goue^{r} Dongan, which waer two to one for ye Eſtwards. He Anſwered he knew, to ye Contrary I An^{ſd} that then Go:^{r} Dongan had ye Mohocks, and Senicaes conſiſting of at Leſt 3 M:[1] men to Send vppon theſe

[1] Three thouſand.

Indeans in ther one ould quarell when he plesed

His Answer was he beleued ye Gou^r^: was mistaken in that two, for he was shuer ye Ffrench Gouo^r^: kept Jesuits: in ye Mohockes Castells and further moer ye ffrench Go:^r^ had Lately sent for ye Mohokes vppon some misdemer and Xecuted Eyght or Nine that ye Mohokes Brought in them selues Alsoe that ye Kenebecke Indeans were Stout ffellows and ffeared not ye Mohocks

---

Council Minutes Indian Affairs.

[Council Minutes v. 66.]

At a Council held at ffort James April 11th 1684.

* * * *

Governor Dongan said he was against giueing any provocation to the Indians, & would use all the faire ways to preserue peace

Governo^r^ Cranfield said that those the province of Mayne had draun themselues into Garrisons

Mr Dudlay replyed it was don by any order from Boſton

Governor Cranfield ſaid there much difference between unneceſſary feare, & many repeated threats & menaces from the Indians & their drawing away yeir wifes

Governor Dongan ſaid that if his officers at Pemaquid did any thing againſt the Indians, beyond his inſtructions, they ſhould ſuffer for it, & that he would not make any preparations to alarum the Indians.

Governor Cranfield propoſed that an allouance ſhould be made wth the Maques to aſſiſt them of Boſton, & the province of Mayne & other Colonies

Gov Dongan anſwered that if any aſſurance came from Boſton & the province of Mayne that the Indians did make warre he would uſe his utmoſt to get the Maquaſe

Governor Cranfield deſired that one might be appointed from N. York Boſton, the province of Mayne & other Colonies to treat about it, to adiuſt the expences wch would be due to the Maques

Governo^{r} Dongan ſaid he was againſt any thing y^{t} might ſhow the leaſt ſuſpition of the Indians, & give them iealouſie

Agreed upon by Cranfield Governo^{r} of the province of Hampſhire, M^{r} Joſeph Dudley & Mr Shrimpton & Governo^{r} Dongan wth the Council that if upon the arrivall of Mr Cranfield into the province of Hampſhire, Mr Dudley & Mr Shrimpton at Boſton they heare of any Acts of Hoſtility com̃itted by the Indians they forthwith giue notice the Governo^{r} of New York who will ſend ſom on purpoſe to them to Conſult what is fitt to be don in it, & to adiuſt the payments that ſhall be due to the Maquaſe for their aſſiſtance in caſe they are employed & further to adviſe & Conſider whatſoever ſhall be neceſſary for the preſervation of his Maties Subjects.

Extract of a letter from Gov Dongan to the Council of the Province of Hampſhire

[Council Minutes v. 68.]

Apr 11. 1684.

* * *

We giue you many thanks for ye kindneſ towards this Governm^{t}, tho we haue no reaſon on o^r^ parts to apprehend a warre wth the Indians; with whom we haue but lately renewed a friendſhip, & haue letters from Pemaquid which mention nothing of any likelyhood of a warre amongſt them, the copy of w^ch^ & ſome other papers are in the hands of ye Governo.^r^

[Council Minutes v. 72.]

At a Council Apr 21^ſt^ 1684

P^r^ſent the Governo^r^
M^r^ ffr fflypſie Mr S. V. Cortlandt
M^r^ L Santer J Spragge

A petition from New Dartmouth for a patent referred untill the Governo^r^ go to Pemaquid

A petition fro^m^ Mr Alleyn for y^e^ ſame referred untill the Governo^r^ go to Pemaquid & both given back to Mr Giles Goddard.

Petition of Inhabitants of New Dartmouth

[New-York Colonial MSS. xxxiv.]

The Humble Petition of ye Inhabitants of ye Towne of New Dartmouth Belonging to his Roy:^{ll} H: James Duke of Yorke, in ye Eaſterne Parts of ye County of Cornhill in America, and to ye Right Hornourable Corn^{ll}: Dongan Govr & Vice Admirall Vnder his Roy^{ll}: High: of New Yorke and its dependences In America wth: ye Reſt of the Honourable Aſſembly Sitting in Councell at ye City of New Yorke. in October Next, &c.

Humbly Sheweth;

That Whereas you^{r} Honours Humble Pettition^{rs}: Obtained a Graunt of a Tract of Land to ſettle it as a Towneſhip about two years Paſt, from the Worſhippfull Henry Joſſlyn Eſq,^{r} Juſtice in Quo: Deceaſed and by virtue of an Order Derived to him from S^{r}: Edmond Androſs, Then Govr: haue Graunted the afforeſ^{d} Inhabitantes To be bounded as ffoll. Viz^{t}: On ye South to ye Sea, On ye North to ye Country, On ye Eaſt wth: y^{e}: River, knoune by ye Name of Damaras Cotte, as alſo w^{th}: y^e: ffreſh Pond, at y^e: head of Said River, and ſo into ye Country, and on ye Weſt bounding Vpon ye Great Iſland of Saccadahoc, and ſo through Bateſmans Gutt, Into y^e: Sea South & by Weſt, and alſo Vpward from Batemans Gutt, Into y^e Country to y^e Great falles, and from thence to great Monſiocage ffalles, and from thence a north and by Weſt Lyne into y^e: Country as p^r Platt will appeare, As alſo y^e: Orridginall Graunt from y^e: above ſaid Joſlyn $Eſq^r$: Whereas yor: $Pettition^{rs}$ Come to vnderſtand from yor: $Hono^{rs}$: hand That all y^e: Inhabitants ſhall haue their Title of Land Confirmed vnto them in Townſhipps, Wee have hearetofore p^rſented yor: $Hono^r$: w^{th}: a Platt of y^e $aforeſ^d$: Toune Bounds as alſo from Vnder y^e $Surveyo^{rs}$: hands, Their Sirveying & Laying out of $ſ^d$: Townſhipp according as y^e Law p^rvides Wee Humbly beſeiching yor: Honour to Graunt & Confirme vnto y^e: now Inhabitants of ſaid Towne all y^e Lands w^{th}: Rivers & Riviletts, Iſlands, & Iletts, Harbours, & Bayes, w^{th}: in y^e: $afforeſ^d$:

Bounds Vnto yo,^{r} Humble Pettition^{rs}: & heires, according to y^{e} Charter of Eaſt Grinoidge, Only Excepting 1^{ſt}, a hundred accres if Demanded p^{r} anum Vnto his Roy^{ll}: Highneſſe p^{r} acknowledgment: w^{ch}: if Graunted & Confirmed by yor Hono^{r}: & Councell, will much Encourage not Onely ye Inhabitants y^{t} are now heare, but others y^{t}: are Comeing if our Lands weare Confirmed Vnto vs, Severall of our Inhabitants are Drawne of already, and others Intend Except they Can haue a ſpedy Confirmation of their Lands made to them

Therefore wee Deſire That yor Honour would be pleaſed to take it into yor ſerious Conſideracõn That a Pattent may be Graunted Vnto vs for our Townſhipp. That wee y^{t}: are heare & others y^{t}: would Come & ſettle amongſt vs may be Encouraged.

Wee doe allſo further p^{r}ſume & make bould to acquaint yor Honour y^{t} wee are Diſturbed by People y^{t} Come heare to Clame Lands by form: & p^{r}tended writes; Capt: Eliſha Hutchinſon of Boſton hath been in theſe Parts, & gives out ſeveare Threttennings y^{t} he will Come & take away our Land wheron our Towne ſtands & ſeverall others Doe Thretten Likewiſe & ſay That they haue more wright to Shew Then wee have to our Lands, Therefore wee deſire y^{t}: yor: Hono^{r}: will Conſider Vs That Wee may haue aſſureance, of our Lands, and y^{t}: no ſuch p^{r}tenders or old Morgages y^{t} were made before the warrs wth ye heathens may be p^{r}ceeded ag^{t}: us: if they ſhould it would Damnifie & vtterly breake vp our Towne: Capt: Hutchiſon ſaith y^{t}: he muſt have Vs become his Tennants or otherwiſe wee ſhall not Live heare.

And allſo when our Repreſentive Mr Gyles, Godward went Laſt; Mr John Allen without ye knowledge of Mr Godward or vs ſent Privetly a Pettition vnto yor Hono^{r}; it being ffalſe as will appeare wee never knew any thing of it vntill Mr Godwards Returne Mr Allen haveing given vp all his former wright & title which he p^{r}tends he had to the neck of Land ye Towne Stands vpon and Elſe wheare, vnder hand & ſeale to vs and willingly tooke a Lott Equall to ye Reſt, as he pretended to Encourage vs to ſettle y^e: Place, as will more fully appeare by ye articles.

Wee Preſume ffurther to aquaint yor: Hono^r: That wee have heare amongſt vs one Capt Nicholas Manning Capt: of a Company That is very Troubleſome, and Doth much Obraide & Diſturbe vs in our buiſeneſſe, Townes Men & Overſeers That are Legually Choſſen by ye Towne he Doth Diſturbe at Publique Meetings, about their Toune affaires, he allſo braggs That his power is better than our's, and ſayth he will ſettle whom he will and where he pleaſe, wch makes Partyes & Diviſions amongſt vs, To our great Trouble, w^ch: if not p^rvented, wee feare will growe worſe, wee Deſireing y^t: yor: Honour will take all matters into Conſideracōn for to graunt vnto vs yor Poore & humble Pettitiones a Confirmacōn of our Lands That wee doe now Enjoy, and alſo y^t yor Honour would be pleaſed for to ſett or nominate ye Name of our Toune according to yo[r] Pleaſure, and what Elſe yo[ur]: Honour ſhall ſee fitting and wee ſhall Euer Pray &c:

ROBERT R FOOT (?)	THOMAS GYLES Juſtice of peace
THOMAS GENT	ELIHU GUNNISON Juſtice of peace
WILLIAM LOVERING his Mark	RICHARD PAIN Maſt maker and Purſar for his Mageſtys vſe in England
CALEB RAY — — —	JAMES COOKE Mariner

[April 21. 1684.]

Commiſſion of Nicholas Manning as Captain of a Foot Company.

[New-York Colonial MSS. xxxiv.]

By the Governor.

Whereas, out of the good opinion I conceiue of You I haue thought fitt to Conſtitute, and appoint you, Cap[t] Nicholas Manning to be Cap[t]. of a foott Company of the militia for the County of Cornwall Theſe are therfore to will and require you to take into your charge and comand the ſaid Company as Cap[t]. accordingly, and Duely to Exerciſe the ſaid officers, and ſouldiers thereof in armes and to your beſt Care and Endeavour, to keepe them in good order and Difcipline, hereby Willing and Requiring them to obey you in all things as their Capt. and you Likewife to obferue and follow, fuch orders and directions as you fhall from time to time Receiue from mee, and for the Doeing this fhall be your Warrant, this to Continue During my Will and Pleafure only; Given under my hand and feale att Fortt James the 28th day of Aprill 1684.

Paffed the Office. THO: DONGAN.

JOHN SPRAGG Sec'y

Commiffion of Gyles Godard as Lieutenant of a Militia Company

[New-York Colonial MSS. xxxiv.]

Thomas Dongan Lievt Governor &c

Whereas out of the good opinion I conceiue of you Gyles Godard I haue thought fitt to Conftitute and appointe you to bee Leiut. of a foot Company of the militia for the County of Cornwall, You are therfore Carefully to Performe the Duty of a Leiut in all things and to

Obſerue ſuch orders as you ſhall from time to time Receiue from your ſaid Cap[t] or other your ſuperior Officers and all Inferior officers and Souldiers of the ſaid Company are to obey you as their Leiu[t] according to the Diſcipline of Warre this Commiſſion to Continue During my Will and Pleaſure only; Given under my hand and Seale the 28: Day of Aprill 1684.

Paſſed the Office THO: DONGAN
J: SPRAGG Sec[r].

A Commiſſion to Caleb Raye for Enſigne after the ſame forme *Mutatis Mutandis*.

Commiſſion of Juſtices of the Peace.

[New-York Colonial MSS. xxxiv.]

By the Governor.

By Virtue of the authority derived unto mee from his Royall High[s]: I doe hereby Conſtitute authorize and appointe you John Allyen, John Dolling, Lawrence Denni, Thomas Giles, Alexander Woldrop, Thomas Sharp, Richard Pattiſhall Eſquires to bee Juſtices of the Peace for the County of Cornwall and Commiſſioners for the ſettling his Royall Highneſſes Territoryes betweene the Riuer Kenebeck and St. Croix Giveing You full Power and authority to act as Juſtices of the Peace, for the Good and Wellfaire of the Government and due adminiſtration of Juſtice, and to Conſult and make Rules and orders, for the Weale and benefitt of his Royall Highneſſe Territories betweene the River Kinebeck and St Croix and to Call to queſtion and puniſh all offenders according to Law, and all Perrſons whom it May Concerne are ſtrictly Charged and Required to give you due Reſpect and obedience accordingly; this Commiſſion is to be of force dureing my Will and Pleaſure, only Given under my hand and ſeale att Fort James this 28: Day of Aprill 1684

Paſſed the Office THO: DONGAN.

J. SPRAGGE Secr

[Council Minutes v. P. 91.]

At a Council held at ffort James July the 9th 1684.

* * *

The petition of the Inhabitants of Pemaquid referred untill the Governo[r] go thither & in the Mean time the former orders to be obſerved.

Orders concerning Block Houſe and the payment of Quit Rents.

[New-York Colonial MSS. xxxiv.]

By the Governor

Ordered that the Block houſe of Merry Meeting bee Imediately Raiſed by the Town of Pemaquid and there to Trade and Traffique Paying Cuſtomes according to the act of aſſembly and the ſaid block houſe to be Raiſed at theire Owne Charge and Likewiſe Enſigne Sharpe is to ſend up to the ſaid blockhouſe one file of men to be Comanded by John Rowden.

And that all veſſells are hereby required to Enter and Cleare att Pemaquid.

Paſſed the Office THO: DONGAN
J SPRAGGE Sec^r^.

Fortt James the 8th day of September 1684.

By the Governor.

Whereas there are Severall Quitt Rents ſtanding out and in arrears to his Royall High^ss^ at Pemaquid Due and Payable ſince the agreement made by the late Governor Sr Edmond Androſs Knight &c Theſe are therefore in his Royall High^ss^ name to authorize Empower and appointe you Allexander Wardrop to aſke demand and Receive all ſuch quitt Rents as are due and Payable to his Royall High^ss^ in the County of Cornwall and to give Receipts for the ſame, for which this ſhall be your ſufficient Warrant. Guen under my hand at Fortt James the 12th day of September 1684.

THO: DONGAN.

You are to Receive all the aforſaid quitt Rents vntill the 26th of Auguſt 1684.

* * *

Commiſſion granted to John Buttery to be Capt of Foott belonging to New Towne and Sackadahock Date the 22^{d} day of October 1684.

Commiſſion Granted to Gyles Godard Eſq^{r} to be Capt of a Foott Company belonging to the Towne of New Dartmouth in the County of Cornwall Date the 22^{d} of Octo 1684.

Commiſſion of Gyles Godard as Surveyor.

Thomas Dongan Lieu^{t} and Governor &c

Whereas by the Severall Petticõns of the Inhabitants of Pemaquid it appears to be Convenient and neceſſary to have a Surveyor in the County of Cornwall I have therefore thought fitt to Conſtitute and appointe Giles Godard Eſq^{r} to be Surveyor of the ſaid County and to Lay out any Tract or Parcell of Land not Exceeding the quantity of one hundred acres for Each Perſon and alſoe to ſurvey all Toune Shippe not already Surveyed not any wayes Prejudiciall to any Perſons

Right or Intereſt and to make a Returne thereof to me for which this ſhall be your Warrant. Given under my hand and ſeale att Fortt James in New Yorke the 22[d] day of October 1684.

Paſſed the Office, THO: DONGAN
J. SPRAGGE Sec[r].

[Council Minutes v. P. 157.]

At a Council June the tenth 1686.

* * *

The Governo[r] propoſed that there being ſom Confuſion amongſt the Inhabitants of Pemaquid, it would be Convenient to ſend Cap[t]. J. Palmer thither to agree wth them for takeing out their patents, & paying of Quitt rents & ordered that Inſtructions ſhould be given to him.

* * *

Licences for the taking up of Land.

[New-York Colonial MSS. xxxiv.]

By the Governor

Whereas John Spragge of this Citty of New Yorke hath deſired my Liberty and Lycence to take up and Enjoye a

Certaine Island Called and Knowne by the name of Summersett Island and the small Island thereunto adjacent Scituate and Lyeing in Pemaquid in the County of Cornwall these may Certifie that the said John Spragge hath hereby Liberty and Lycence granted to him to take up and enjoy the said Islands in order for Confirmation by Pattent Provided the same be not appropriated or dispossed off to any others Given under my hand at Fortt James in New York:

THO: DONGAN

By the Governor.

Whereas James Graham of the citty of New Yorke Merchant hath desired my Liberty and Lycence to Take up and Enjoye one thousand acres of Land scituate Lyeing and being in Pemaquid in the County of Cornwall, These may Certifie that the said James Graham hath hereby Lyberty and Lycence granted to him to Take up one thousand acres of Land provided that not aboue one hundred acres of the said land be fronting to the sea or water side also provided the ſame be not appropriated or legally diſpoſed of to any others. Given under my hand at Fortt James in New Yorke the 19th day of June 1686

THO: DONGAN.

By the Governor.

Whereas Thomas Smyth Gent. hath deſired my Lyberty and Lycence to take up and Enjoye three hundred Acres of Land Scituate and Lyeing in Pemaquid Theſe may Certifie that the ſaid Thomas Smyth hath hereby Lyberty and Lycence to take up the ſaid three hundred acre of Land in Order for Confirmation by Pattent Provided the ſame be not appropriated or Legally Diſpoſed of to any others Given under my hand at Fortt James in New Yorke the 19th day of June 1686.

THO: DONGAN

By the Governor.

Whereas Thomas Cooper of the Citty of New Yorke Gent. hath deſired my Liberty and Lycence to take up and Enjoye three hundred acre of Land Scituate Lyeing and being in Pemaquid in the

County of Cornwall These may Certifie that the said Thomas Cooper hath hereby Liberty and Lycence to take up the said three hundred acre Provided the same be not appropriated or Legally disposed of to any others, Given under my hand att Fortt James in New-Yorke the 19th day of June 1686.

THO: DONGAN.

Authority of John West to act as Deputy Secretary.

[New-York Colonial MSS. xxxiv.]

Forasmuch as it hath Pleased the Right Honble: Coll Tho Dongan his Majestyes Gouernor of New Yorke & to Commissionate and Empower Capt John Palmer of the Citty of New Yorke Esqr by grant or Deed in writeing vnder his hand and seale of the Prouince to Give Grant Rattifie and Confirme to all and Euery the Persons in Pemaquid now Settled and Inhabiting within that Partt of his Majestyes Prouince as shall be Desirous to take up settle and appropriate Land there, ſuch tract and tracts Parcell and Parcells and quantities of Land and Iſlands as in his Diſcretion he ſhall think moſt fitt and Conuenient I do hereby nominate and appoint and depute you John Weſt of the Citty of New Yorke Gen^t to doe and Execute all act and acts thing and things in Pemaquid in the County of Cornwall dureing the time that Capt John Palmer ſhall ſtay in the ſaid County to my office or Place of Secretary belonging or apperteining

Given under my hand and at Fortt James this 19th day of June 1686.

J: SPRAGGE Secr.

Commiſſion of Capt John Palmer

[New-York Colonial MSS. xxxiii.]

By the Governor in Councill.

Haveing Receiued information that there be Seuerall diſorders and Confuſions amongſt the Inhabitants of Pemaquid I haue therefore thought it conuenient to ſend you Capt John Palmer thither of whoſe great Prudence abilityes, and Integrities I am Very well aſſured.

And for the better Eſtabliſhing Settling and quietting of his Majeſtyes ſubjects in thoſe Parts, in their Eſtates and Poſſeſſions I doe hereby giue you full Power and authority to treate with the ſaid Inhabitants for Takeing out Pattents and Paying the quitt rents.

And to Preuent any dangers that may ariſe by being in a negligent, vnprovided Poſture you are to warne the aforeſaid Inhabitants to keep in Garriſon Continually one officer and ſix ſouldiers at Leaſt in time of greateſt Peace and quiett and twenty Souldiers at Leaſt if any warr ſhould ariſe & happen.

And for the more Regularly Proceeding in all affaires you are hereby alſoe Empowered to nominate and Chuſe diſcret and honeſt Perſons ſome of the moſt knowing and Capable Perſons to be Justices of the Peace and quorum.

And foraſmuch as very Little Reuenue hath accrued to his Majeſty from Pemaquid by the Dutyes of Exciſe and Cuſtomes you are therefore hereby Impowered to Sett and Lett to farme the aforeſaid Exciſe & Cuſtomes as advantagiouſly as you Poſſibly can, for the augmenting of his Majeſtyes Reuenue.

And Laſtly you haue hereby full Power and authority not only to act in the afore-ſaid Perticulers but in any other concerne or thing what ſhall be moſt meet and convenient for his Majeſtyes Intereſt.

Giuen under my hand and Seale at fortt James in New Yorke the 19th day of June 1686.

THO. DONGAN

Commiſſion of Juſtices of the Peace for Cornwall County.

[New-York Colonial MSS. xxxiii.]

Cornwall SS.

James the Second by the Grace of God of England Scotland Ffrance & Ireland King Defendr of the faith Supream Lord of ye Plantacōn & Collony of New York To our Truſty & Wellbeloved, Tho Sharpe, Richard Patiſhall, Tho. Giles, Nico. Manning Giles Goddard, Jno Dolling, Laurence Denny, Elihu Guniſon Eſqrs Greeting. Know yee That wee haue aſſigned you & Euery of you Joyntly &

ſeverally our Juſtices to Keep our peace within our County of Cornwall in o^{r} Plantation & Collony of New York Aforeſ^{d} And to keep & Cauſe to be Kept all thoſe laws & ſtatutes made & Eſta-bliſhed for ye good of ye peace & for ye Conſeruacõn of the Same & for ye quiet Rule & Gouermn^{t}. of our people within o^{r} S^{d} County in all & Singular their Ar-ticles according to ye force forme & Effect thereof, Ant to Correct & Puniſh all offenders ag^{t}. the forme of ye Laws & ſtatutes or either of them in ye County aforeſ^{d} as according to ye forme of ye Laws or Statutes is or ought to be done. And to Cauſe to Come before yo^{u} or either of yo^{u}. all thoſe who Doe threaten any of o^{r} People concerneing their bodies or of burning their houſes to find ſufficient ſuretyes for ye Peace & their good beha-viour towards us & our people & if they ſhall refuſe to find Security in this behalfe then to Cauſe them to be kept ſafety in our Priſons untill they ſhall find ſecurity in this behalfe.

Alſoe wee aſſigne yo^{u} & Euery three or more of yo^{u} whereof any one of yo^{u}, you[u] ye[e] aforesd Tho: Sharpe, Richard Patishall Tho: Giles, & Nic[o] Manning wee will to be one our Justices to Enquire by the Oaths of good & Lawfull men of ye[e] County aforesd[d] by whom ye[e] truth of the thing may be the better Knowne for all manner of Larceny Petty Larcenay Trespasses & Extortions whatsoever & of all & singular other misdeeds Crymes & Offences of the which ye[e] Justices of our peace may or aught Lawfully to Enquire by whomsoever & howsoever in ye[e] County aforesd[d] done or perpetrated or w[ch] hereafter there shall happen to be done or Accompted where the punishment thereof by the Laws of the s[d] Collony doth not Extend to taking away of Life limb or member. & alsoe of all those who there doe lye in waite to wound or Kill our people or that hereafter shall soe presume to lye in Waite And alsoe of all p[r]sons that shall & doe use & sell by false weights or measures. And also of whatsoeuer Sherriffs Brayliffs Marshalls Constables Goalers & other officers who in the Execution of their offices ab[t] the p[r]misses or either of them haue behaued themselues undutyfully or hereafter ſhall p^{r}ſume to behaue himſelfe undutifully or are remiſſe or negligent or hereafter ſhall ſoe happen to be in ye County aforeſ^{d} & of all & ſingular Articles & Circumſtances & other things whatſoeuer by whomſoeuer & howſoeuer in ye County aforeſ^{d} done or perpetrated or wch hereafter there howſoeuer ſhall happen to be done or Attempted concerning the full truth of ye p^{r}miſſes or any of them & to Inſpect whatſoeuer Indictm^{ts} ſoe before yo^{u} or any of yo^{u} taken or to be taken, or before others late Juſtices of ye peace in ye County aforeſ^{d} done or taken & not yet Ended And to Continue proceſſe thereupon ag^{t} all & ſingular perſons ſoe Indicted or whom before yo^{u} hereafter ſhall happen to be Indicted untill they are taken Deliuer up themſelues or be Outlawed. And to heare and determine all & ſingular ye Larcenys Petty Larcenys Treſpaſſes Extortions Indictm^{ts} aforeſ^{d} & all & ſingular ye prmiſſes according to ye Laus of y^{e} ſ^{d} Collony as in Caſes of this nature is uſed or ought to be done, And to Correct & puniſh the Offend^{rs} & euery of them for their offences by fines & amercements, or otherwiſe as according to ye Laws of ye ſd Collony is uſed or ought to be done

And alſoe we Aſſigne you and every three or more of you whereof any one of you the aforeſd Tho Sharpe Richard Patiſhall Tho: Giles & Nico Manning Wee will to be one of our Juſtices to heare try & determine by the oaths of twelue good and Lawfull men of ye County aforeſd all Cauſes & Caſes there brought & Commenced before you as well accōns Caſes & Cauſes Civill between Party & party as Criminall of which ye Juſtices of ye Peace in their Seſſions by the Laws of ye ſd Collony may & ought to heare try & determine & in ſuch manner & forme as by the ſd Law is prſcribed & Directed.

Provided always that if upon the Determinacōn of any of ye prmiſſes or Caſe of Difficulty ſhall happen to come before you or any three or more of you that then you doe not proced to giue Judgmt thereupon (unleſſe in ye prſence of one of our Juſtices of or Court of Oyer & Terminer within our ſd Collony) And therefore wee Command you & Every of you that you

Dilligently Attend ab^{t} the Keeping of ye Peace Laws & all & ſingular other ye p^{r}miſſes and that at certaine days & places which by o^{r} Leiut & Governor of o^{r} ſ^{d} Plantation & Collony of N Yorke for that purpoſe ſhall be appointed yo^{u} make Inquiry of ye p^{r}miſſes & all & ſingular ye p^{r}miſſes heare & determine & to doe & accompliſh thoſe things thereupon in forme aforeſ^{d} to be done wch appertaines to Juſtice according to ye Lawes & Cuſtomes of our ſ^{d} Collony ſauing to us our ffines & Amerciam^{ts} & other things to us thereupon belonging.

Alſo we command by Vertue of theſe p^{r}ſents our Sheriffe of our ſ^{d} County of Cornwall that at Certaine dayes and places (which ſhall be appointed & made Knowne unto him as aforeſ^{d}) he Cauſe to come before yo^{u} or any three or more of yo^{u} as in ſaid ſuch & ſoe many good & Lawfull men of his Baylwick by whom ye truth in ye p^{r}miſſes may be the better knowne & Inquired off. In Teſtimony whereof we haue Cauſed y^{e} ſeale of o^{r} ſ^{d} Collony to be hereunto Affixed. Wittneſſe Jno Palmer Eſq of ye Councell in o^{r} ſ^{d} Collony & Commiſſion^{r} for y^{e} ſettling of our Affaires & Appointing of Juſtices of ye Peace in o^{r} ſ^{d} County the Eighth day of Septemb^{r} in y^{e} ſecond yeare of our Reigne Annoq Dom. 1686.

The Oath of a Juſtice of the Peace.

Y^{e} ſhall ſwear that as Juſtices of the peace in ye County of Cornwall in all articles in the kings Commiſſion to yo^{u} directed yo^{u} ſhall doe equall right to ye poore & to ye Rich after yor Cuning Witt & power, & after ye Laws of ye Collony thereof made. And yo^{u} ſhall not bee of Counſell of any Quarrell hanging before yo^{u} & that yo^{u} hold yor Seſſions after the forme of Law thereof made & att times & places appointed And the ffines & Amerciaments that ſhall happen to be made & all forfeitures wch ſhall fall before yo^{u} yo^{u} ſhall Cauſe to be Entered without any Concealm^{t} or Imbezelling & truly giue them to his Maties Deputy Collector and receiver in y^{e} ſ^{d} County for the time being or ſend them to his Maties Collector & receiuer Generall att New Yorke or to his Maties Court of Exchequer there Ye ſhall not Lett for Gift or other Cauſe but well & truly yo^u ſhall doe yor office of Juſtice of ye peace in that behalfe & that yo^u take nothing for yor office of Juſtice of the Peace to be done but yor ffees accuſtomed & Lymitted by Law. And y^e ſhall not direct or cauſe to be directed any warrant by yo^u to be mad^e to ye partyes but yo^u ſhall direct them to ye Sherriffe of y^e ſ^d County or other the Kings officers or Miniſters or other Indifferent perſons to doe Execucōn thereof.

Soe help yo^u God &c

Inſtructions for Capt Nicholas Manning Sub-Collector Surveyo^r and Searcher of his Maties Cuſtomes and Exciſe due & payable in ye County of Cornwall & Receiuer of his Maties Quittrents & other reuenues arriſeing within y^e ſ^d County.

[New-York Colonial MSS. xxxiii.]

Impri^s. You are to take notice of all ſhipps and veſſells whatſoever comeing to any porte within y^e ſ^d County & ſee that they make Juſt & true Entryes and that Immediately upon their Arriull both of Veſſell & Goods.

2dly You ſhall keep a true & p'fect account of all monyes by you receued on goods in Lieue thereof for his Maties Cuſtomes & Exciſe.

Enter ye Names of all veſſells & the Names of ye Maſters in a Diſtinct booke by you to be kept for that purpoſe

3dly. You ſhall not p'mitt any ſhip or Veſſell whatſoeuer directly or Indirectly to Load nor Unload any goods wares or Merchandize untill ye ſd Ship or Veſſell hath firſt made her due Entry inward or outward

4thly. You ſhall appoint certaine Convenient place or places at which & noe other goods may be Shipped or Landed & that at Seaſonable times between ſun riſeing & ſun ſetting in ye day time & in p'ſence of an officer

5thly You ſhall from time to time dureing your being in ſd office Returne to ye Governor or his Maties Collector & Receiuer Generall for the time being att New Yorke a true & Juſt account of what yo^{u} haue receiued & Collected & of yor Proceeding in yor ſ^{d} Office once euery ſix months att ye furthereſt

6^{thly}. You are to Collect & receiue his Maties Cuſtoms & Exciſe in ye County of Cornwall aforeſ^{d} according to an act of Eſtabliſhm^{t} therefor made by the Generall Aſſembly & publiſhed the 31. October 1683.

7^{thly}. You are to goe into ye houſe & Cellar of any p^{r}ſon or p^{r}ſons whatſoeuer where y^{e} ſuſpect there is any wine or other Liquors & ord^{r} the ſ^{d} Liquors to be Gauged Cauſeing them to pay for all Rum ſoe found in ye Cellar & they who ſhall ſell by retaile to pay for all Liquors Wines beere & Syder that ſhall be by them ſold & retailed. You are alſoe to goe into their Cellars & houſes as aforeſ^{d} as yo^{u} ſhall ſee Cauſe to p^{r}vent all fraud & Imbezellment of his Maties Reuenue.

8^{thly}. You are not to ſuffer any Veſſell whatſoever to goe into or up Kenebeque River or any parte thereof untill they haue firſt made their Entry with yo^{u} at Jameſtown & payed his Maties Dews & if any ſhall prſume to doe ye Contrary y^{o}

are to Cauſe both veſſell & Goods to be Seized & proceeded agſ^{t} by Law as directed for defrauding his Matie of his Cuſtomes

And that all Veſſells tradeing into any porte River or place doe Enter & Cleere with yo^{u} before their departure und^{r} the like pains & forfeitures.

9^{thly} You are to take Care that ye former Ord^{rs} made Relateing to ye ffiſhery be duly obſerved & that what Ordred to be payed by all ſtrange veſſells & Shallops Coming to make their voyages in theſe parts be by yo^{u} duly Collected for his Maties uſe of wch account to be likewiſe giuen as afore directed

10^{thly}. You are not to ſuffer any p^{r}ſon or p^{r}ſons to ſell any ſorte of Liquors by retaile in any part or place within y^{e} ſ^{d} County but ſuch as ſhall obtaine Lycence from yo^{r}ſelfe & ſhall pay ſuch ſume of mony for ye Same as yo^{u} ſhall think fitt to agree for & not Leſſe than 12^{s} for Each Lycence g^{r}ted and of ye Monys on that behalfe receiued yo^{u} are to Render a p^{r}ticuler ac^{t} to ye Govr as opportunity p^{r}ſents.

11thly You are to Collect & receiue ye Quitt rents due & payable from ye Severall persons for ye Lands they hold within ye sd County according to a List of Pattents granted Left with you in ye Speties therein menconed & thereof to Keep a Distinct account & alsoe of all fines forfeitures & amerciaments that shall or may at any time hereafter happen or belong to his Matie & thereof to send an act to ye Governor or his Maties Receiuer Generall att New Yorke for ye time being once euery 6 months att furtherest.

12thly. In Case any prson Licenced to sell Liquors by Retaile desire ye same you may farme the Excise of their Draught to them for one yeare for such sume of money as you shall think fitt to Agree for haueing regard to ye greatnesse of their Draught.

13thly. You are to write to ye Gouernor or his Maties Collector or Receiuer Generall att New Yorke for ye time being of all passages Concerning the Excise, Customes Quitt rents & other his Maties Reuenue to ye End that suitable Ordrs may be from time to time sent you for regulateing ye same.

14thly. ffor yor Better Governm^t^ in Collecting of ye Customes & Excise aforesd you haue herewith a Breviar of ye Act of Generall Assembly Establishing ye same And these Direccons you are to follow & obserue untill further Ords. Dated att Jamestown in ye County of Cornwall the 17th day of 7bler in ye second yeare of his Maties Reigne Annoqe Dom 1686

Confirmation of Roswick or Arrowsick Island to John West

[Patents vi. 30.]

Thomas Dongan Capt: Genll: Governor: in Chiefe and Vice Admirall in and over the Province of New Yorke and Territoryes Depending thereon in America under his most Sacred Majesty James the Second by the Grace of God of England, Scottland, ffrance and Ireland King Defender of the faith &c To all whom these prsents shall Come Sendeth Greeting Whereas John Palmer Esqr by Virtue of the Commiccon and authority unto him by me Given by a Certaine Grant under his hand writing the ſeale of this Province thereto affixed and entered of Record in the Secretaryes office bearing Date the fifth *Day* of Auguſt in the Second Yeare of his ſ[d]: Majeſtyes Reigne and in the Yeare of our Lord one thouſand Six hundred Eighty Six hath Given Granted Rattified and Confirmed unto John Weſt of the Citty of New Yorke in America Gentl All that Certaine Tract or Parcell of Land or Iſland Scituate Lyeing and being on the Eaſt ſide of Kenebeck als Kenebeque River within the County of Cornwall Commonly called or knowne by the Name or Names of Roſwick or Arrowſick Iſland according to the furtheſt Bounds limitts and extents thereof as the ſame is Encompaſſed by Water together w[th]: all and ſingular the Meſſuages Tenements Edifices Buildings, Trees, Timber Woods underwoods ffields ffeedings Paſtures Moores Marſhes Swamps Meadows Ponds Pooles Lakes Streams Rivers Runns Rivoletts Waters and Water Courſes ffiſhing fowling hawking and hunting with the Privilidge of Building and

Erecting Saw Mills or Griſt Mills thereon or on any Parte thereof and all other Privilidges imunityes Profitts benefitts advantages Hereditamts: and appurtennces whatſoever to the ſaid Tract or Parcell of Land or Iſland and Premiſſes belonging or to or with them or any of them in any wiſe appurteineing Alwayes Excepted and Reſerved out of the ſaid Grant all that Peece or Parcell of Land Parte of the ſaid Iſland at the South end thereof formerly Granted by Sr: Edmund Andros Knight late Governour of this Province unto Mr Lawrence Dennis & others Inhabitants there Called by the name of New Towne, to Have and to hold the ſaid Tract or Parcell of Land or Iſland and all and Singular other the Premiſſes with their and Every of their appurtennces Except before Excepted unto the ſaid John Weſt his Heires and Aſſignes *to* the Sole and only Proper uſe benefitt and behoofe of the ſaid John Weſt his Heires and Aſſignes forever under ſuch Rents and Services as in the ſaid Grant are mencõned and Reſerved as in and by the ſaid Grant Relacõn yrunto being had may more fully and att Large Appeare.

Now Know yee that by virtue of the Commiſſion and authority unto me Given by his moſt Sacred Majeſty our now Soverigne Lord James the ſecond aforeſaid & Power in me Being and Reſideing for and in Conſideracõn of the Rents and Services herein after Mencõned and Reſerved I have Given Granted Ratified Releaſed and Confirmed and by theſe Preſents Doe Give Grant Rattifie Releaſe and Confirme unto the ſaid John Weſt his Heires and Aſſignes for ever all that the above recited Tract or Parcell of Land or Iſland and Premiſſes with all and Singular the Hereditam[ts] and appurtennces thereunto belonging or appertaineing in as full and ample manner as the ſame is mencõned to be Granted unto him by the ſaid John Palmer Except what in the ſaid Grant is Perticulerly Excepted and Reſerved to have and to hold the ſaid Tract or Parcell of Land or Iſland and Premiſſes with their and every of their Appurtennces Except before Excepted unto the ſaid John Weſt his Heires and Aſſignes to the Sole and only Proper uſe beneffitt and behoofe of him the ſaid

John West his Heires and Assignes forever Yielding Rendring and Paying therefore Yearly & every Yeare unto his most Sacred Majesty his Heires & Successors forever or to such Officer or Officers as from time to time shall be Empowered to Receive the *same* the sume of twenty Shillings Currant Mony of New Yorke in Lieu and Stead of all Rents Services Dues Dutyes and Demands whatsoever, to be holden of his most Sacred Majesty his Heires and Successors in free and common soccage according to the Tenure of East Greenwich in the County of Kent in his Majestyes Kingdom of England:

In Testimony of the Premissess I have Caused these Presents to be Entred and Recorded in the Secretaryes Office and the Seale of this his Majestyes Province to be hereunto affixed the sixth day of December in the second yeare of his said Majestyes Reigne, and in the yeare of our Lord God one thousand six hundred and Eighty Six.

THOMAS DONGAN.

May it Pleaſe your Excellency.

The Attorney Generall hath Peruſed this Pattent and finds nothing Contained therein Prejudicall to his Maties Intereſt.

JA: GRAHAM.

Exam^d^ 9^m^ber 30th 1686.

Att a Councill held att ffort James the ſixth day of December 1686.

Preſent His Excellency the Governour.
Major Antho: Brockholls.
Mr Fredrick Fflipſon.
Mr Steph V. Courtland.
Mr John Spragge
Major Gervis Baxter.

This Pattent was approved off

J. SWINTON Clk Councill.

Royal Order for the Surrender of Pemaquid to Maſſachuſetts

[Deeds viii—75]

James R.

Truſty & well beloved wee Greet you well. Whereas wee have thought fitt to direct that our ffort & Country of Pemaquid in Regard of its diſtance from New Yorke bee for the future annexed to & Continued under the Governm^{t} of our territory & dominion of New England our will & pleaſure is that you forthwith Deliver or cauſe to be delivered our ſaid ffort & Country of Pemaquid with the Greate Gunns[1] ammunicōn & ſtores of warr together with all other vtenſills & appurtennces belonging to the ſaid ffort into the hands of our truſty & welbeloved Sr Edmund Androſs Knight our Captaine Generall & Governour in Cheife of our territory & dominion of New England or to the Governour or Commander in Cheife there for the time being or to ſuch perſon or perſons as they ſhall Impower to receiue the ſame and for ſoe doing this ſhall be your warr^{tt}.

Given at our Court at Windſor this 19th day of Septr 1686 & in the ſecond yeare of our Reigne.

By his Maties Comand
SUNDERLAND Cl.

[1] The Great Guns from the Fort at Pemaquid, after being carried to Boſton, were by order of the King in the spring of 1691, transferred to New York. (N. Y. Coll. MSS. xxxvii.)

Remonſtrance againſt Surrender of Pemaquid &c.

[Council Minutes v. 221.]

Council Held at ffort James Wednſday ye 28th of March 1688

* * * *

Reſolved that an adreſs to his Maj^{tie} be Drawn up giveing his Maj^{tie} an account that this Goverment has bin much Diminiſhed by takeing away Pemaquid the Jerſeys Penſylvania and the three Lower Countys of Delawar. That this is the Bulwarke of all theſe partes of America that the Revenue is but ſmall yett the Charges very great.

That Connetticut in his Maj^{ties} Pattent from Chares y^e 2^d is added to Boſton by y^e Contrivance of the $Governo^r$ of it & the Clerke of the Collony & unknown to y^e Major parte of y^e Collony

That y^e ffrench warr has Stopt y^e beaver trade ſo y^t without ſome ſpeedy help this place will be Ruined.

Notices of Indian Hoſtilities

[New-York Colonial MSS. xxxvii.]

Extract from a letter of John Eaſton of Rhode Iſland to Col Henry Sloughter Governor of New York; dated June 24. 1691.

* * * *

Wee have intelligence that the Eaſtward indians & ſome ffrench have made an aſault vpon y[e] gariſons in and neere the Towne of Wells and have killed about ſix perſons therabout. They drove their Cattell together & killed them before their faces.

* * *

Notice of Capture of Pemaquid by French and Indians

[Council Minutes vii. 213.]

At a Councel held at his Maties ffort in New Yorke the 23th of Auguſt 1696.

* * * * *

His Excell did Communicate intelligence from Boſton that the two ffrench Shipps that took the Newport Galley with the aſſiſtance of the Indians have taken Pemaquid ffort & that it is reported by one of the Capts that Count ffrontenac has orders to take Albany & Schenectady with intelligence of a great Squadron of Ships lately ſeen upon the coaſt of Jamaica.

* * * * *

Paſſes.

[Paſſ Book—iv.]

Diſpatch granted to the Barke Elizabeth Alizander Woodrop Maſter bound for Pemaquid November: ye 29th: 83.

Diſpatch granted to the Sloope Happy Returne James Barry Commander for Pemaquid & New found Land Aprill 26th 1684.

Diſpatch granted to the Sloope Bloſſum Stephen Heacock Co͂mander for Pemaquid May the 22^{d} 1685.

Diſpatch granted to the Sloope Primroſe John Eureſt Maſter for Stratford and off Pemaquid New Yorke July the 4th 1685.

Diſpatch granted to the ſleoop Lewis Francis Baſſett Co͂mander for Pemaquid & New found Land [Sept 4 (?) 1685.]

Dispatch granted to the Sloope Adventurer Thomas Brookes Commander for Boston & Pemaquid, June 19th 1686

Lucas Andries· Mafr of the sloop Elias Enters the sd sloop for Pemaquid with Contents of Loading. [June 20. 1681.]

Lawrence Sluce Enters the sloop Hopewell himselfe Master ffor Pemquid with Contents of Loading. [Sept 10. 1681.]

Stephen Hiskott mar of the Sloop Blossome Enters the sd Sloop for Pemaquid with Contents of Loading [Oct 21. 1681.]

www.ingramcontent.com/pod-product-compliance
Lightning Source LLC
LaVergne TN
LVHW021409110826
845150LV00007B/1849

* 9 7 8 1 4 2 5 5 1 1 5 3 1 *